LONDON

past and present

Text
Chiara Libero

Editing Supervision by
Valeria Manferto De Fabianis

Art Director
Patrizia Balocco Lovisetti

Graphic Supervision by
Anna Galliani

Translation by
Neil Frazer Davenport

*1 In London
the symbols of power
are to be found
everywhere, even in
this sculpture on the
banks of the Thames.*

*2 and 7
The frontispiece of
The Illustrated
London News, a
nineteenth-century
periodical, provides
us with an image of a
wealthy London
prospering, thanks to
its trade with all four
corners of the world.
However, behind this
facade lay a very
different city: the
London described by
Dickens and
Disraeli.*

*3-6 A view of the
City from the
Thames. The new
skyscrapers rise
alongside the symbols
of political power and
religious faith.
The name of the river
that divides the city
in two derives from
the Celtic teme.
Throughout the long
history of London the
Thames has been one
of its principal
arteries of
communication.*

This edition published in 1997 by TIGER
BOOKS INTERNATIONAL PLC , 26a York
Street Twickenham TW1 3LJ, England.

First published by Edizioni White Star.
Title of the original edition:
Londra.
© World copyright 1997 by Edizioni White Star,
Via Candido Sassone 22/24, 13100
Vercelli, Italy.

ISBN 1-85501-903-5

Printed in Italy by Grafedit, Bergamo (Italy).
Colour separations by Magenta Lithographic Con.,
Singapore and Fotomec, Turin (Italy).

CONTENTS

10 top and 10-11 A bright red Routemaster double-decker bus, one of the best know symbols of London. The old buses with their rear platforms and spiral staircases are gradually being replaced by new models that lack one of the city's most characteristic figures: *the bus conductor who asks passengers' destinations, takes their fares and issues tickets. Now it is the driver himself who is responsible for all these duties. However, a trip on the top deck of a Routemaster is still one of the most enjoyable parts of a stay in London.*

Eastern spices, however, are nothing new to British cookery (in Thackeray's *Vanity Fair* the cowardly Jos offers forward little Becky Sharp a chilli pepper, making her swoon) and tea has of course long been adopted as a Great British emblem. In modern day London it is perhaps easier to find exotic delicacies than good old English roast beef.

This does not mean that the city has been transformed into a Jamaican market, but it is indicative of how a place that in the collective imagination is formal and restrained is able to accept and exploit even radical changes. The empire and its role as arbiter of the global chess board having been lost — the duties being handed over not without regret to Washington and New York — London and the rest of Great Britain has experienced long, difficult periods of economic and social crisis.

What has in part saved her is language: the English of London is by no means the same as the English spoken on the other side of the Atlantic, but it is taught well.

The English language school business is enormous and brings with it an even greater prize. Just think of the hundreds and thousands of student who, each year, arrive here from throughout Europe, Asia and Africa. They are all looking for lodgings, they all eat in the fast food joints and they all spend rivers of sterling in the schools for foreigners. The most dili-

gent spend their Saturdays and Sundays in the museums, the night people among them frequent the discotheques and virtually all of them return home with the idea that London is, potentially, the world's greatest city.

And who are we to say they are wrong? While it might not be as beautiful as Rome or Paris, as intriguing as Prague or as outrageous as New York, London really is a fascinating place in which to live.

11 top A solitary carriage heading for Buckingham Palace. Alongside the aristocratic London, still clinging to its ancient traditions, there is another city all bustle and modernity. There is thus room both for the old-school coachman with top hat and tails and modern bus drivers and cabbies of diverse ethnic origins.

11 bottom A member of the Queen's Life Guards in service at the Tower of London. The various guards regiments play a fundamental role in the complex ceremonies that punctuate the daily routines of the city's great monuments. At the Tower of London, for example, the Ceremony of the Keys is performed each evening to close the gates after the last "stranger" has left.

*12 top Big Ben is not,
as many believe, the
name of the bell tower
of the Houses
of Parliament, but
of the great 14-ton
bell itself that tolls
the hours. The nick-
name comes from
Sir Benjamin Hall
who was Commissioner
of Works when the bell
was hung in 1858.
Big Ben is the second
bell to be hung in
tower as the first was
cracked during
trials. The clock itself
is also of particular
interest: it is the
largest in the United
Kingdom and even
in the digital age its
accuracy is proverbial.*

The Sixties, with the explosion of Swinging London, youth fashion, excessive make-up and revolutionary music, gave rise to a modern myth that, in spite of being around for at least two decades, still survives. London has managed to export throughout the world lifestyles, clothes, music and the illusion that the city is there for the taking just by walking down Oxford Street dressed in a mini-skirt and beads. The fact that the Londoners over twenty-five years of age looked askance at the multi-coloured crowd convinced of their power to change the world with love and peace was not important. The blows to the economy and the welfare state sustained during the Thatcher years dented the illusion to some extent, but it has failed to dim the appeal of the city in the eyes of those who love her. Evenings in the pubs, afternoons in the Victoria and Albert Museum library handling precious manuscripts under the paternal gaze of the guard. Sunday morning strolls through the Regent's Park rose garden. Harrods' sales. The market at Brixton with its mysterious fruits and magical herbs. Whole days browsing in bookshops in search of the ghost of Edith Sitwell or in hunting down an elusive art book. A greeting to Peter Pan and another to Boadicea. The families that provide board and lodgings for students and live any of the myriad suburban outposts linked by the underground system, only occasionally visit the city centre, rarely go to the West End theatres and inhabit their own microcosm centred around a tube station, a church — or synagogue, mosque, temple or chapel — a post office and a main road with shops and banks. They are far removed from the town planners' earnest discussions of the Docklands renaissance, from the sociologists' treatises on the punks or Soho's red light district and from the connoisseurs' arguments over the influence of ethnic cooking on Old English cuisine. They may never have been to the National Gallery but they are perfectly up-to-date on the latest Royal scandals blown out of all proportion by the media. They have very little in common with the Mayfair aristocracy and the Bond Street shops, with the gentlemen's clubs or the affairs of the city. And yet they too are Londoners, born and bred.

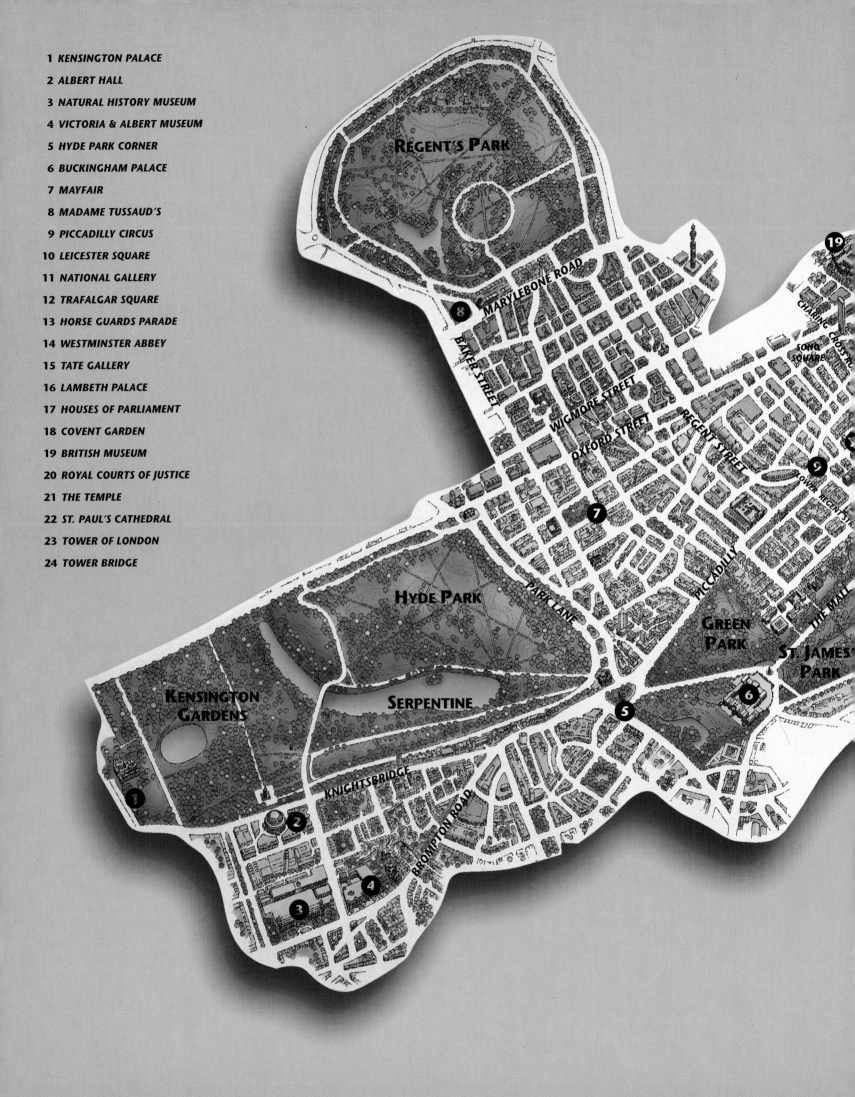

HIGH HOLBORN

FLEET STREET

QUEEN VICTORIA ST

LONDON BRIDGE

RIVER THAMES

STRAND

EMBANKMENT

VICTORIA

WHITEHALL

WESTMINSTER BRIDGE

Westminster, the seat of parliament.

Piccadilly Circus.

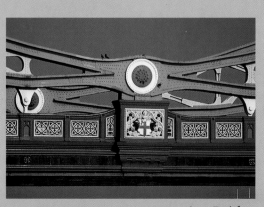

London Bridge.

20-21 *A map of Londinium Augusta, Roman London. The name probably derived from the Celtic term* Llyn-din *meaning the "fortress near the lake", and the original settlement consisted of wooden huts principally used to house livestock. The choice of site on which* to found the city was apparently dictated by the fact that here the river could be easily forded whilst access to the sea was close to hand. Quays allowed ships for the transport of troops and goods to be moored. The map reproduced here clearly shows the grid *pattern typical of Roman cities with streets intersecting at right-angles surrounded by a wall. Important roads led out from the centre to other Roman cities established on the island: the present day Bath, Colchester, York, Chester, Exeter and Canterbury.*

I t has to be said, even London was a Roman invention. Prior to the conquest of the island, Londinium was probably a Celtic village, Llyn-din. The Romans' choice of site was virtually inevitable as at this point the Thames was easily fordable and the vicinity of the sea eased the problems of trade and communications with the rest of the empire. Londinium was a prosperous and extensive settlement by the standards of the day, with temples, a basilica, workshops and a necropolis. The Roman domination suffered a severe setback thanks to the efforts of one remarkable woman, Boadicea or Boudicca, the Queen of the Iceni. The story is well worth telling: Boadicea, the widow of King Prasutagus, attempted to accede to her husband's throne. The conquerors, however, made it quite clear that her minor kingdom was of no importance in the great imperial scheme of things other than as land to be appropriated. This they did with such arrogance that Boadicea rallied her troops and led a revolt. The Romans eventually quelled the uprising, but the fearless Queen had the satisfaction of sacking the wooden Roman village located more or less where London Bridge stands today. Londinium was reconstructed: it was a town grouped around a wooden bridge, with warehouses for goods, homes and a temple dedicated to Mithras. Those interested in archaeology will find the remains of Roman walls not far from the Tower of London, whilst entire mosaics have emerged in the City, together with relics that can be admired in the British Museum and the Museum of London.

In part at least, the most important London streets follow the routes of the great Roman roads: Oxford Street leads to the West, the long Mile End Road to the East and Old Kent Road to the South. London developed into a commercial and administrative jewel under the Emperor Augustus, but it was not to last.

20 top This small statue, found in the waters of the Thames, depicts an Egyptian divinity adopted by the Romans and imported into their lands of conquest.

20 bottom Boadicea, the courageous and legendary Queen of the Iceni, led a rebellion against the Roman invaders and sacked the city of Londinium. The illustration is taken from a work by Meyrick and Smith dedicated to the customs of the inhabitants of the British Isles (1815).

21 top A bronze bust of Hadrian, found in the Thames at London, and a coin minted during his reign, bear witness to the success of the Roman expeditions following the conquest of Britain by Julius Caesar in 55 and 54 BC. The Emperor Hadrian sponsored the construction of the "vallum" (known as Hadrian's Wall), the moat around the empire designed to protect it from marauding tribes.

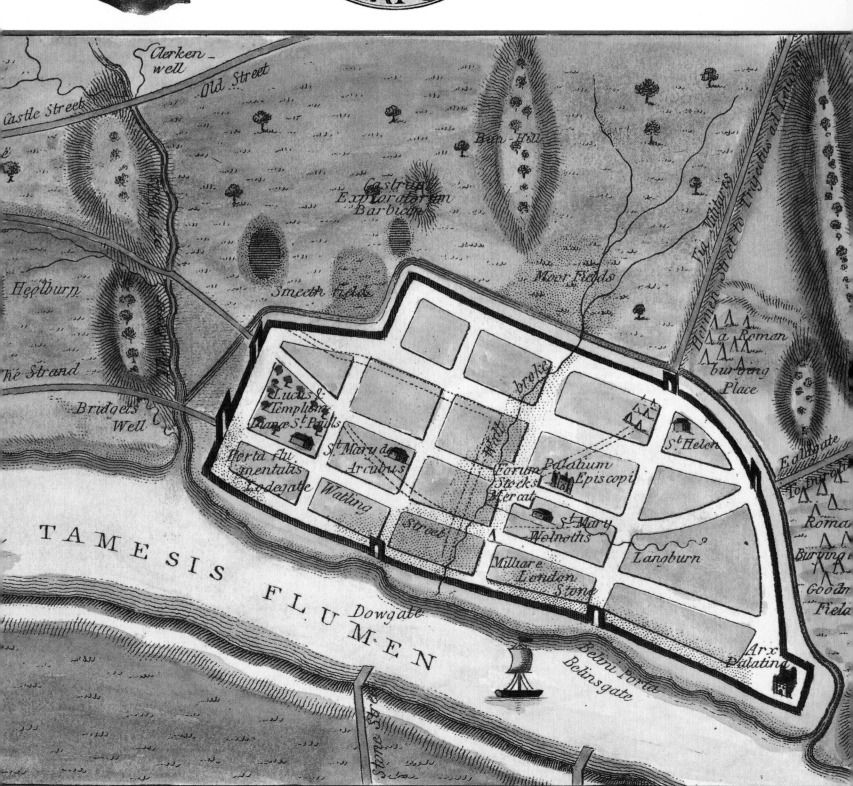

The decline began in 410 AD, not only for Londinium, but for the whole of Roman Britain. The imperial capital was obliged to recall its garrisons to the continental mainland to defend itself against the Germanic hordes and left to its own devices the colony sank into a long period of decay.
During the dark ages the city fell into the hands

K. EDWARD the CONFESSOR.

To the most High Puissant DUKE of NORFOLK &c. by his Grace's most Obedient and Noble Prince EDWARD This Plate is humbly Inscrib'd humble Servant. J. Mechell.

of the Saxons and acquired a certain importance thanks in part to the spread of Christianity. At the end of the sixth century, when Pope Gregory I appointed the future Saint Augustine as Archbishop of Canterbury, London was defined by the Venerable Bede as "the market of the world". It was soon to be given a cathedral, St. Paul's, and became a see in 604. London was, however, still a provincial settlement confined by the borders established by the Romans. The great urban expansion got underway in 1042 with the accession to throne of Edward the Confessor, the last Saxon King, Edward transferred the royal seat to a monastery on Thorney Island, Westminster Abbey, where all his successors were to be crowned, married and eventually buried.

23 top An episode in the life of Hengist, the Anglo-Saxon leader who is said to have colonised the kingdom of Kent.

23 bottom left A miniature executed in the Benedictine San Gallo monastery depicting Saint Gregory the Great who sent a group of monks to Britain. The group was headed by Augustine, the future Archbishop of Canterbury.

23 bottom right Ethelbert, the King of Kent and the author of the first Anglo-Saxon legal code, was baptised by Saint Augustine.

24 top The Queen Matilda Tapestry conserved in the Bayeux Museum depicts the Norman conquest of England in 58 scenes. The scene on the left portrays William the Conqueror whilst that on the right shows the sovereign and his fleet attacking Dinan on the French coast.

24-25 The French infantry repelling the Norman attack. This was an episode that bears little resemblance to the real events: on the 14th of October, 1066, the infantry could do little to stop the Norman cavalry. The political and military skills of William the Conqueror had already been revealed in his homeland where, at a still very young age, he had succeeded in putting down a baronial rebellion and in gaining the protection and support of the Church.

25 top In a contemporary miniature, the final phase of William the Conqueror's victorious campaign to unite the kingdoms of Normandy and England under his rule: this is the Battle of Hastings (1066) during which William defeated the English forces led by

Harold of Wessex. In order to legitimise his operation William carried with him the vexillum sancti Petri, that is to say a sacred banner sent to him by the Pope. With this he could claim the protection and support of the Holy See of which he declared himself a servant.

25 bottom William's victory in the Battle of Hastings was celebrated with a banquet illustrated in one of the scenes of the Queen Matilda tapestry and, above all, by the crowning of William on the 25th of December, 1066 at Westminster.

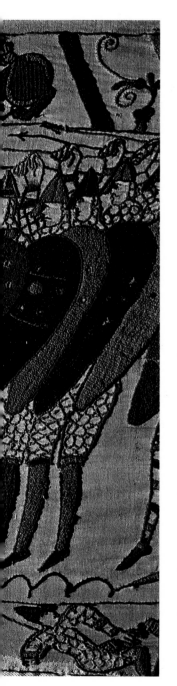

The importance of the western area of the city increased with the arrival of the Normans and the reign of William the Conqueror. William boosted urban development with the construction of a powerful fortress, the White Tower that is now part of the Tower of London, but above all he provided the city with a privileged administrative structure with an elected mayor flanked by counts.

Expansion along the right-hand bank of the Thames began thanks to the construction of the stone-built London Bridge and trade continued to prosper. Goods arrived via the river and bartering took place in the narrow, tortuous streets that replaced the regular Roman plan and are still a characteristic feature of the oldest part of the city. The new St. Paul's cathedral was the religious centre of London and oversaw numerous parish churches. Trading colonies from the continent were established in the city, with groups of Danes, Dutchmen, Italians and Germans.

London also housed Jewish bankers who were, however, stripped of their goods in the late eighteenth century and thrown out of the city, their place being taken by Italians. In 1215 the Magna Carta was signed by King John; the document guaranteed the guilds' great municipal autonomy: "the city of London shall retain all its ancient liberties and customs".

26 top right. John Lackland hunting deer in a miniature from 1315 conserved in the British Museum. When the King obtained the annulment of the Magna Carta Libertatum from the Pope, the barons rebelled and offered the English throne to Prince Louis of France.

26 top left The Magna Carta Libertatum was signed at Runneymede on the 15th of June 1215, by King John Lackland.

The Charter defined the feudal rights of the barons, the liberties of the Church and the English cities and the civil rights of all free citizens.

26 bottom A facsimile of the Magna Carta Libertatum reproducing the passage regarding the barons. The monarchy was to be controlled by a body composed of twenty-five barons. Further clauses guaranteed the feudal rights of succession and the right of every free man to be judged by a court of his peers.

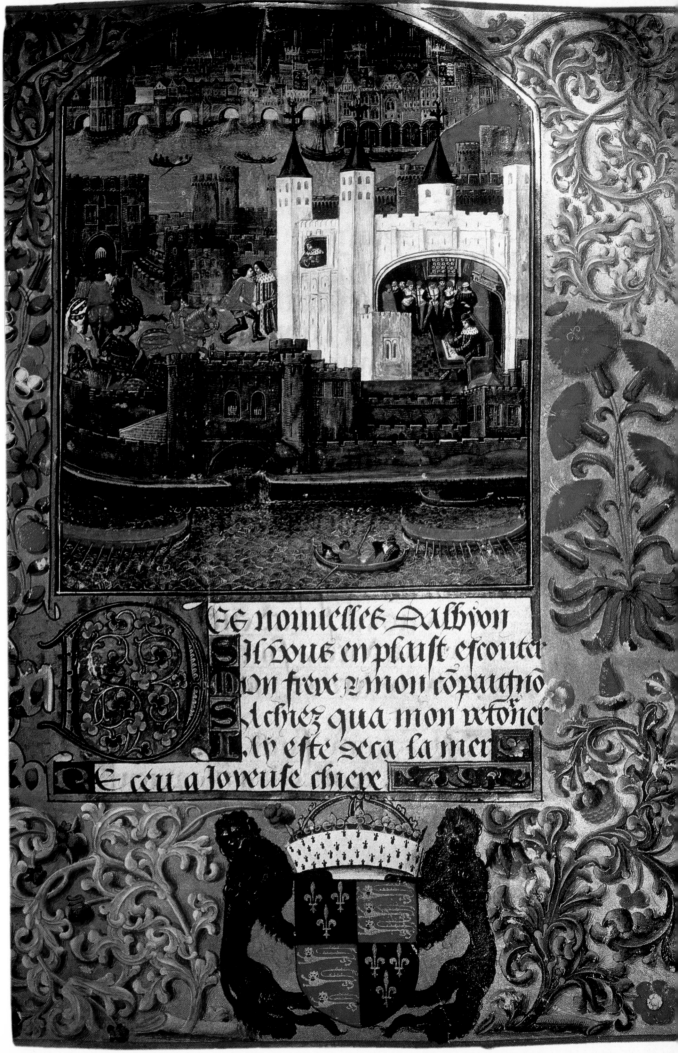

27 This miniature, taken from a book of the 15th century, shows a view of London with the White Tower. The tower was completed in 1097 under the aegis of William the Conqueror and is the central keep of the Tower of London. Since Norman times it has been used variously as a royal zoo, a storehouse and a prison. Today the appearance of the building reflects the modifications made by the architect Christopher Wren in the 18th century. On the ground floor is the ironically nick-named "Little Ease", an extremely small, windowless cell in which the worst criminals were detained. The spiral staircase in the North-East turret rises in an anti-clockwise direction to allow defenders to use their swords in their right hands.

coin alquant, pisan: ... e p...
i gambacozli e be... magioz... signoz... ... ch ... ...
come fu mona grande

28 top A dramatic illustration of the plague that ravaged Europe in 1348 without sparing London.

28 centre In 1381 a great mob marched on London to protest against the taxes destined to finance the Hundred Years' War. This miniature shows Richard II sailing on the Thames to meet the rebels at Rotherhithe.

28 bottom The assassination of Wat Tyler, the leader of the Peasants' Revolt (a miniature taken from the Chronicle of English History from the 15th century). The episode aroused the wrath of Richard II.

London's prosperity was dealt a severe blow in 1348. The plague, the Black Death, fell upon the city in an era in which it was home to over 50,000 people and in which wealth was in the hands of those controlling trade. There was little incentive for expansion and the inclusion of new, fresh forces and the interests of the inhabitants of the old inner circle prevailed over the reality of the situation. A few decades later, in 1381, the Peasants' Revolt saw the uprising of a great number of underprivileged citizens hit by the taxes imposed to pay for the Hundred Years' War with France

and the various military offensives that England undertook on the continent.

The rebellion was short-lived but it posed a serious threat to the *status quo* and even went as far as endangering the safety of the archbishop. Following this brief uprising, feudal order was restored and the increasingly powerful merchants celebrated their position of absolute economic privilege with the construction of the Guildhall in 1440. This symbol of mercantile power still exists and still features in the ceremony of the "silent exchange" in which the Lord Mayor of London receives the symbols of his office.

29 The revolt of 1381 gave rise to numerous episodes that inflamed the popular spirit such as the preaching of John Ball (top picture) and the killing of the Archbishop of Canterbury (bottom picture).

The young king did all he could to restore peace, negotiating with the rebels and sweetening them with promises and concessions. However, his every initiative was soon nullified by the intervention of parliament. With his prestige seriously dented, Richard II attempted a coup d'état but was defeated by the aristocracy led by Thomas of Gloucester.

vant ce vint le ven dredy au matin ce peuple qui eftoit logie en la place Sainte Kathe rine devant la tour du chaftel

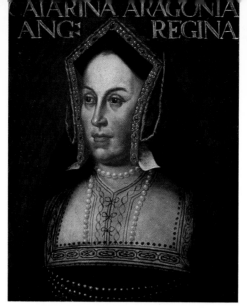

30 top Catherine of Aragon, (left) and Anne Boleyn (right) were the first two wives of Henry VIII.

30 centre The Anglican reformation led to the English crown's break with the Church of Rome.

30 bottom Henry VIII has earned a place in history thanks to his bloody marital affairs:

after Catherine of Aragon and Anne Boleyn he married Jane Seymour, Anne of Cleves, Catherine Howard and Catherine Parr.

30-31 Early in his reign Henry VIII (here with the Archbishop Sherbourne) had assumed anti-Lutheran positions, to the extent that he was appointed by the Pope as a defensor fidei, or Defender of the Faith.

In spite of the increase in its population, London remained a typically medieval city, still largely confined within the Roman walls. The peasants that arrived from the countryside were forced to live in miserable conditions and there thus arose a need to extend the city limits. At last the city centre was allowed to expand and a form of local government was set up with the creation of the county. A London was about to be born that in general terms we can still recognise today. It was to be a king ·followed by an extraordinary queen who were to determine the city's future layout. London and England's golden age was in fact marked by the reigns of a great sovereign, Henry VIII, and his even more significant daughter, Elizabeth I.

Henry VIII is considered by many historians and town planners to be the true founder of modern London: the reform of 1536 that saw the secession from the Church of Rome and the creation of the Church of England, was also the occasion of an important urban transformation. The dissolution of the monasteries made available a great deal of land and property that the sovereign proceeded to hand over as gifts and to sell to his favourites and supporters. London thus began to expand beyond the now obsolete confines of the City and Westminster, whilst many religious buildings were converted and transformed into hospices, orphanages, refuges for old people and prisons.

31 top left Martin Luther, seen here in a portrait by Lucas Cranach, was principally responsible for the secession of the western church.

31 top right This illustration shows Henry VIII's petition for divorce from his first wife.

32 Two contemporary prints showing the Tower of London, a veritable citadel composed of a number of buildings. The structure was begun by William the Conqueror following the Battle of Hastings and was intended to be a military fortress on a strategic site on the banks of the river just outside the city walls. In the centre can be seen the White Tower, the ancient nucleus. The Tower of London was used as a Royal Palace up to the reign of James I as its architectural features made it extremely secure. Today the Tower houses the Crown Jewels and one of the world's most spectacular armouries. According to various legends, numerous ghosts roam the Tower, the spirits of those executed during its long history.

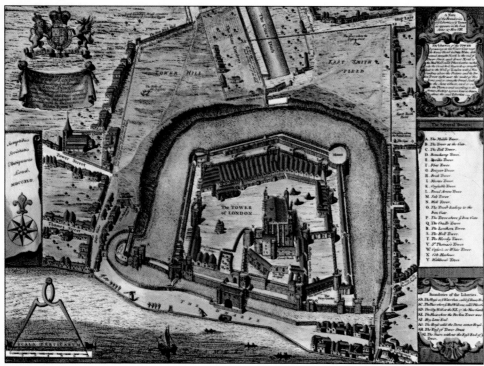

32-33 A map of London from the 16th century. As you can see, the area to the South of the Thames was almost completely undeveloped. On the right can be seen the imposing bulk of the Tower of London, just past London Bridge and the City, the oldest part of the metropolis.

33 top left The Customs house in a water-colour by Bartholomew Howlett from 1663. Three years later, the complex was destroyed, together with much of the city, in the Great Fire of London.

33 top right London Bridge in the era of Elizabeth I. In 1967 the old bridge was sold to an American company for two and a half million dollars. It was then dismantled and rebuilt, brick by brick, in Arizona.

34 top A map of London in 1640, taken from the Atlas Novus. During the reign of Elizabeth I, the population of the city increased from 50,000 to over 200,000.

34 centre Elizabeth I, in a celebrated portrait by Marcus Geeraerts the Younger. The Queen, who came to the throne in 1558 at 27 years of age, governed with energy and determination and the era identified with her name was characterised by the presence of great artists and illustrious writers.

34 bottom Westminster Hall was the place where Oliver Cromwell was proclaimed Lord Protector in 1653, exactly the same place where Charles I had been sentenced to death.

The work continued with Elizabeth's accession to the throne, and by the early XVII century London was composed of three distinct parts: the old City that had retained its role as an economic and trading centre and also contained the homes of the citizens, Westminster which along with the St. James estate (the royal deer park) was the seat of political power and the brand-new quarter of Southwark that was built on land confiscated from the church and became a modern "industrial zone". The city was by now a seething anthill: between 1530 and 1600 the population within the city walls numbered 75,000, but no less than 150,000 lived in the suburbs where craft industries were flourishing in the fields of silk, glass and ceramics. Great commercial monopolies such as the Moscow, Levant and East India Companies were also created, favoured by maritime conquests. This was the era of Shakespeare who, in order to side-step a mayoral edict prohibiting theatrical productions in the city, sought out a suitable site to the South. The Globe, one of the world's most celebrated theatres was built at the southern end of London Bridge. The building of Covent Garden, initiated by the Duke of Bedford, followed shortly afterwards: a regular street plan in contrast with the labyrinth old City, buildings echoing the styles of Renaissance Italy, open spaces, quarters located around a square with areas dedicated to commerce, religion and society. The piazzas developed in the seventeenth century can still be seen today: Leicester Square, Soho Square, St James's Square.

The architect who had the greatest influence on the city's new direction was Inigo Jones, a devotee of Andrea Palladio and the author of the design for the Covent Garden complex.

35 top William Shakespeare was born at Stratford-upon-Avon and arrived in London at the end of the 16th century.

35 bottom left Inigo Jones, the architect, in a portrait by Dobson. Having returned to England in 1605 following a stay in Denmark, Jones began to work for Queen Anne and King James I. Only seven of his works survive today to bear witness to his love of Italian art and architecture.

35 bottom right The Globe Theatre in a water-colour by James Stowe. As the mayor and the city council had banned theatrical performances from the city, the new theatre was built on the south bank of the Thames.

Paradoxically, two great tragedies were responsible for further developments in the city's urban planning.

In 1664 a chronic lack of water and the paucity of the contemporary hygiene provisions led to a new plague epidemic (and the death of around 100,000 inhabitants) followed by a devastating fire that swept away much of London. Once the flames had been brought under control 13,000 buildings and 87 churches were found to have been destroyed. The Great Fire of London proved, however, to be a remarkable opportunity for the archi-

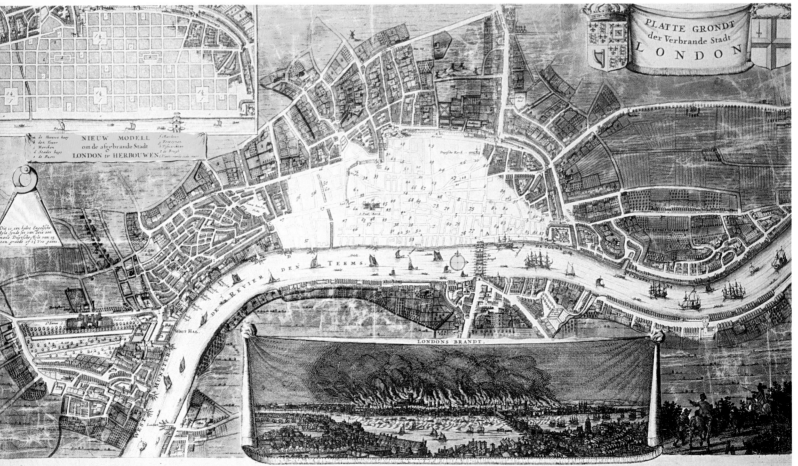

Afbeelding van de
STADT LONDON.

Representation curieuse de l'embrasement de la
VILLE de LONDRES,

Delineation of the
CITIE LONDON,

36 top A print taken from the frontispiece of a book of the mid-17th century describing the tragedy *of the plague that struck the city and the surrounding area. The illustration shows the dead being* *given a decent burial in London and being thrown into a common grave in the countryside.* *36 bottom London and the Great Fire of 1666 that started in a baker's shop in Pudding Lane* *and caused the destruction of 13,000 houses and 87 parish churches.*

37 left Sir Christopher Wren, the Superintendent of Works and the leader of the committee responsible for the reconstruction of the city following the Great Fire, in a portrait by John Closterman.

The architect prepared grandiose designs intended to lend the centre of London a more solemn atmosphere but his ideas were adopted only in part.

37 bottom right Mansion House, the official residence of the Lord Mayor of London, was designed by George Dance.

37 top right Christopher Wren's original design for St. Paul's Cathedral. The great dome in white marble was intended to rise above all other buildings. The building was rightly considered to be the architect's masterpiece and was built on a site that had been sacred to Londoners since the 7th century.

tect Sir Christopher Wren, the General Superintendent to the Crown, who was responsible for the reconstruction of the city. Wren had grandiose ideas and immediately began planning a very different city with airy, spacious squares and broad avenues. Unfortunately he was baulked by the proverbial British traditionalism and the need to rebuild quickly. He was however commissioned to rebuild 51 churches, first and foremost among which was his masterpiece, the new St. Paul's. The urgency of the rebuilding programme led to a demographic expansion that in turn encouraged the construction of buildings in the West End, new bridges over the Thames — Westminster, Blackfriars, Battersea — and new suburbs on the south bank. The creation of the Bank of England in 1694 provided the wealthy bourgeois merchants with a formidable instrument. Those with the means to do so fled the overcrowding of the East End and new working class quarters were created.

38-39 A contemporary print of Leicester Square in 1751. The harmonious geometry of the square is unrecognisable today, encroached upon as it is by cinemas, night clubs and young people looking for entertainment. The transformation took place in 1874 when a speculator decided to alter the 18th-century plan that had featured a large garden surrounded by railings.

39 top A panoramic view of London in 1750. One can see London Bridge and the dome of St. Paul's Cathedral. The West End began to expand in this period and New Road, extending the Oxford Street route northwards, was completed. This was an important innovation that led to further expansion of the city. In the same era the Bloomsbury quarter was created and the numerous villages that had sprung up around the old nucleus began to be joined together.

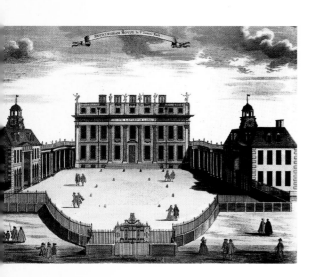

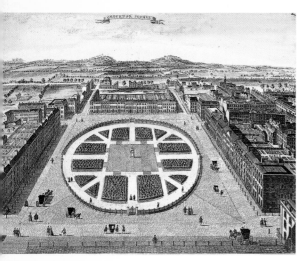

By the eighteenth century, London could boast around 750,000 inhabitants. Immigrants arrived from Ireland and Europe. In the meantime Great Britain had assumed a leading role in global trade, dominating the seas and establishing colonies. Thus began the golden age of London architecture, financed by mercantile trade, with residential quarters constructed on the great estates of influential Whig and Tory families: Hanover Square, Bedford Square, Russell Square.

The city centre was embellished with sublime architectural crescents such as those designed by John Nash.

A typical example is Regent Street, linking the elegant, exclusive St. James's area with the new Regent's Park development. Nash was also responsible for initiating work on what was to become Trafalgar Square and for beginning Buckingham Palace. Under his influence, great public buildings such as the National Gallery, the British Museum and the arch at Hyde Park Corner were constructed in the Neo-Classical style.

This was the London in which Thackeray set his *Vanity Fair*; a lively city full of opportunity for those like Becky Sharpe who had their wits about them and in complete contrast to the somnolent countryside.

38 top An engraving showing Buckingham Palace as it appeared early in the 18th century. At that time the building belonged to the Duke of Buckingham, John Sheffield, who had married the daughter of James II. The brick-built edifice featured wings linked to the central block by colonnades.

38 bottom Grosvenor Square in the heart of Mayfair was built, like many other developments such as Hanover Square, Piccadilly and Berkeley Square, as a result of property speculation that followed the Great Fire and continued throughout the 18th century.

40 top left
The commercial importance of the city expanded greatly thanks to its trading relations with the rest of the world and by the end of the century it was calculated the docks extended for almost a hundred kilometres. Today merchant ships no longer arrive in the Pool of London, but the Docklands revival project is bringing the area back to life.

40 bottom left
In 1760 Covent Garden Market belonged, as it still does today, to the Duke of Bedford. This was the first London district to be built according to a rational town plan. Until 1974 it housed the wholesale fruit, vegetable and flower markets. In the background can be seen the church of St. Paul designed by Inigo Jones in the "Greek" style and adopted as the actors' church. Today the area is a lively agglomeration of shops, stalls and small antique shops.

40 right A print of Ludgate Hill in the 19th century. In that era the residential areas of the City were being replaced by office buildings and the inhabitants were evicted. The arrival of the railways in the heart of the city exacerbated this situation. The viaducts penetrated a maze of busy, narrow streets strewn with straw, where workers, housewives and hawkers all jostled for space among the carriages and omnibuses.

41 A painting by Canaletto showing the procession of the Knights of the Order of the Bath in front of Westminster Abbey. The Abbey is a splendid example of Gothic architecture and was consecrated in 1269. Subsequently it was subjected to a series of modifications whilst still remaining one of the symbols of the British Crown. Here princes become kings and princesses queens, here royal weddings are celebrated and here the sovereigns rest, side by side with illustrious artists and writers.

This wealth and development were not felt throughout London however. If on the one hand there were areas in which luxury appeared to be the norm, on the other there were hive-like workers' districts constructed to house the great wave of labour attracted by the nascent industrial revolution. In 1821 there were 1,140,000 Londoners, a veritable army in expansion thanks to the flood of immigrants. London was the world's financial capital and it was its stock exchange that determined the fluctuations in the prices of primary materials. The needs of industry also affected the urban structure and the city expanded exponentially; the inhabitants of the City, overrun by offices, commercial buildings and warehouses, were obliged to abandon their old homes. To allow both blue and white collar workers to reach their work-places, a railway network was constructed that, whilst very advanced for its era, left great scars in the historic heart of London. A contemporary print reveals what life must have been like in the City: below the Ludgate Hill viaduct, in view of the dome of St. Paul's, wagons and carts, potato sellers, gentlemen in top hats and commoners swarm in a confusion anything but attractive. The creation of the artificial dock basins changed out of all recognition the districts lining the banks of the Thames.

42-43 *London between the 17th and 18th centuries, painted by Jan Griffier (hanging in the Sabauda Gallery, Turin). At that time the Thames was still one of the principal means of communication.*

44 top Victoria, seen here in a photograph by Alex Bassano, became Queen at just 18 years of age and during the early years of her reign she was advised by Lord Melbourne. In 1890, the year of this portrait, Queen Victoria had already been on the throne for 53 years and she was to remain there until 1901 before giving way to her son, Edward VII. An energetic, strong-willed woman, observant of conventions, it is said that she had just one weakness, her beloved husband Albert of Saxe-Coburg-Gotha with whom she had nine children.

44 bottom Thanks to the support of Queen Victoria, Benjamin Disraeli, the leader of the Tories, succeeded in passing an electoral reform that established the right to vote for all householders and £10 rent payers in the cities, thus doubling the numbers of voters. Disraeli, who was also a respected writer, polemicist and satirist, also worked to improve the conditions of the working class, taking an interest in public health and the right to strike.

44 centre In this painting by David Roberts, Queen Victoria is seen arriving at the ceremony of the opening of Parliament. The scene is repeated, with few changes, in the present day: the Queen travels to Westminster in a ceremonial carriage, escorted along the Mall by the Royal Cavalry.

Beyond its superficial wealth, the London of Queen Victoria (who reigned from 1837 to 1901) showed all the signs of a community that had grown too far too fast. The novels of Charles Dickens denounced the inhumane conditions of the orphanages, the prisons and the workers' housing and his works helped to accelerate the adoption of measures to defend the weaker members of society. Pollution also contributed to a worsening of conditions, with the air dense with the smoke of factories, workshops and domestic chimneys. A dense smog is described by Dickens in one of the most celebrated passages in *Bleak House*. In this period many other writers, artists and politicians took up London's cause ("Jaws of hell, monster, metropolis of the empire" wrote Cobbett in 1821). In 1854 Benjamin Disraeli, for example, published the novel *Sybil, or the Two Nations* in which he spoke in forthright terms of the gulf between the worlds of the rich and the poor. Late in the nineteenth century Ebeneezer Howard's name was indelibly linked with a new direction in town planning, the garden cities. Taking advantage of new transportation systems, Londoners were to be encouraged to emigrate beyond the smog and the sprawl of offices, houses and factories and its mass of malcontent humanity.

45 top A 19th-century sectional view of Charing Cross station. The creation of the London Underground, commonly known as the Tube, dates back to the middle of the 19th century.
The first line was inaugurated in March, 1863, in the middle of the Victorian era. The last, the Jubilee Line, was opened on the occasion of Elizabeth II's silver jubilee. The network is therefore a collection of extremely modern stations and others that still retain a 19th-century air, garish colour schemes and old cast iron structures. In spite of the size of the system (it is the most extensive in the world), the eleven lines form a network that is relatively easy to understand and use: each line is distinguished by a different colour and the stylised tube map is a familiar London symbol reproduced on everything from mugs to T-shirts.

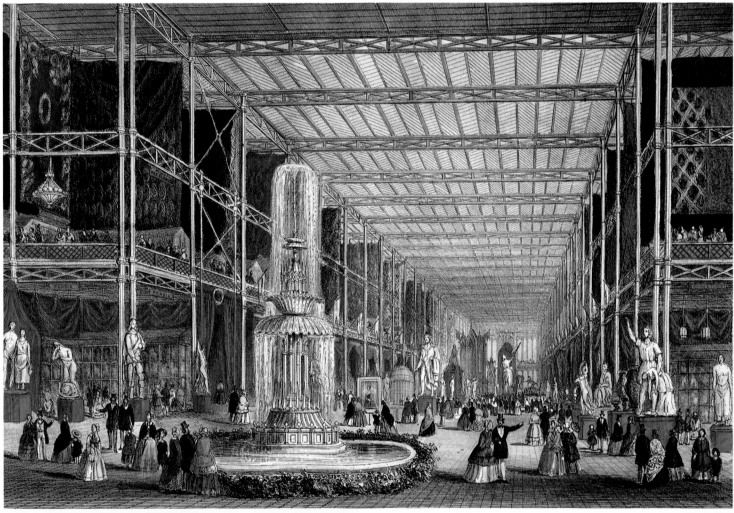

45 centre The Great Exhibition of 1851 was the first in history worthy of the name. Promoted by Queen Victoria and above all by Prince Albert, it was inaugurated in the presence of 30,000 guests in the great glass building, the Crystal Palace, erected in Hyde Park. The event was an authentic triumph for the Empire which thus celebrated its power and supremacy in the fields of industry and technology. By the time the exhibition closed it was calculated that 700,000 people was passed through the turnstiles from all parts of the kingdom and throughout the world.

45 bottom The name of Ebenezer Howard is linked with the concept of the garden city, an alternative to the chaos of the frenetic metropolitan life. The prototype of this new form of city was Letchworth, built to the North of London in 1903 by Howard himself and the architect Raymond Unwin.

46 top The old Westminster Bridge dated back to 1749 and was replaced in 1862 by a structure designed by Thomas Page and Charles Barry. The grey-painted ironwork, the elegant lamp-posts and its vicinity to the temples of faith and politics made London's second oldest bridge one of the most evocative locations in the city.

46-47 The original site of the Royal Exchange, founded in 1565 by Sir Thomas Gresham, was in a courtyard where merchants bartered their goods, a tradition for a city that had been a centre of trade since its foundation.

*47 top
This contemporary print shows a carriage passing the Coliseum at Regent's Park. This area was designed as an out-lying park with a number of villas and a palace for the Prince Regent.*

47 centre Behind this severe Neo-Classical facade lies the temple of learning of the era, London University.

47 bottom In the 17th century, Leicester Square was one of the most fashionable areas of London; in the 19th century,

it became known for its clubs and places of entertainment; in the 20th century it is still central to the capital's lively night-life.

48 *This contemporary print shows a delightful cross-section of London life of the 19th century. Heavy carriage traffic animates the street flanking the Central Post Office, whilst in the background the moon illuminates the dome of St. Paul's.*

49 The customs houses of London docks served one of the country's busiest ports. The city's trading vocation led, over the course of the centuries, to the construction of great warehouses, those which today are being transformed into apartments for the young lions of the City as part of a massive rebuilding scheme.

In 1901 London had a population of around 5 million. The suburbs extended almost endlessly with dormitory towns composed of thousands of single-family terraced dwellings with their pocket handkerchief backyards or gardens. The demand for housing led the city centre to be neglected and it remained practically unchanged up until the end of the Second World War. The intense traffic was in part absorbed by the underground railways that were electrified in 1890 and linked to the surface network.

The consequences were considerable, especially from a social point of view. London was no longer simply a city in the usual sense of the term, but as the geographer Geddes was to say it had become a "conurbation", a collection of radically different urban centres linked by a web of metropolitan trains, buses and taxis. In the meantime the decentralisation of industry removed the factories and workshops to peripheral areas where

50 bottom Edward VII and his wife Princess Alexandra of Denmark. The photograph dates from 1903: the King was 62 years old and had been on the throne for just two years. An unrepentant Don Juan and bon vivant, a lover of fine food and beautiful women, Edward was the complete opposite of his mother, a severe moral guardian who frequently complained about his style of life, most unfitting for a future sovereign.

51 top The Royal
Exchange and the
Bank of England
in an image of
bygone times when
all the bankers
and humble office
staff wore dark suits
and bowler hats,
and never forgot
their umbrellas.

51 centre Ludgate
Circus and Ludgate
Hill in the heart
of the city with
St. Paul's Cathedral

in the background.
The chaotic traffic
has been joined
by advertising
hoardings.

51 bottom Cannon
Street derives its
name from
candlestick, as when
the commercial
activities of the
City were still
in their early days,
and candle makers
lived and worked in
this area.

overheads were lower. The problem of housing was tackled through a combination of private (the Peabody and Guinness Trusts for example) and public financing. The London of the early twentieth century was also home to a number of great literary and cultural figures from Virginia Woolf, the fulcrum of the Bloomsbury Group, to Forster, from Eliot to Auden, from the passionate art critic Roger Fry to craft enterprises such as the Omega Workshops. After centuries of splendid isolation, political events and the war on the continent obliged Great Britain to reassess its position, as alternative markets such as New York began to replace London at the head of world trade. At the same

time, the British government also had to cope with the dominions' thirst for independence inspired by growing nationalistic fervour. The great London, the centre of the world, was experiencing one of the most difficult periods in its history. The mass unemployment that followed the depression of '29 (three million people were left without work throughout the country), the decline of the traditional industries such as coal mining and the independence of much of Ireland were all factors that had a particular effect on the capital. In the aftermath of the Second World War, the city was left facing an even more urgent problem, that of reconstruction.

52 top and centre Tower Bridge in flames (top), St. Paul's Cathedral (top left) and the Houses of Parliament (right) were involved in the heavy Luftwaffe bombing of June, 1941. A total of 29,000 people were killed by the bombs and the appearance of London was changed for ever.

52 bottom left Sir Winston Churchill visiting the city after the bombing of September, 1940; in the June of the same year Churchill had been named as Prime Minister in place of Chamberlain.

The public saw Churchill as a strong, determined figure capable of standing up to the Nazi threat. In fact, having abandoned his initial position of tolerance towards Mussolini's Fascist Italy, and

aware of the danger represented by Hitler's Third Reich, Churchill had promised to rearm Great Britain and established close alliances with the United States and the Soviet Union.

In 1944 the Plan for the London Region (integrated twenty years later with the Greater London Development Plan) attempted to impose a more rational structure on the development of the city. The devastation caused by the German bombing campaign was only one of the problems facing the authorities charged with the task of determining the direction in which this immense urban agglomeration was to move. It appeared of fundamental importance to establish a green belt and to decentralise as much as possible in favour of the New Towns, satellite communities built around the principal hub in open countryside. In the city centre much was invested in the reconstruction of the damaged buildings and the road network, but also in the restructuring of public spaces: one compromise between the old and the new that has attracted almost unanimous approval is Covent Garden, a redeveloped area in the heart of London that allows people to see a show, eat, shop and meet each other within an attractive urban environment.

*53 bottom left
The Coronation
Coach, built in 1762
to the design of the
architect William
Chambers, carrying
Queen Elizabeth II
back to Buckingham
Palace following the
ceremony at
Westminster Abbey.
It was the 2nd of
June, 1953, the new
Queen was just 27
years of age and had
been on the throne for
16 months following
the death of her
father George VI.*

53 top left Sir Winston Churchill during the 1945 electoral campaign. Victory in the Second World War failed to guarantee political *success for Churchill in the post-war years. The great statesman did not, however, retire from public life and continued to act as the leader of the* *opposition. He also devoted himself to writing and his historical works earned him the 1953 Nobel Prize for literature.*

53 right The Queen and the Prince Consort, Philip Duke of Edinburgh, saluting her subjects from the balcony at *Buckingham Palace. The Queen is wearing the Imperial State Crown containing 2,800 diamonds as well as other jewels.*

54 Three symbols of the Sixties that transformed London into a paradise for whole generations of young people, who gathered in the old imperial capital from all over the world in search of music and freedom. The Beatles (top, in a scene from the film A Hard Day's Night, 1964), Mary Quant, the woman who officially "invented" the miniskirt (centre, during the presentation of a collection of shoes in 1967) and, bottom, Carnaby Street, the street of fashion and excess par excellence.

One could hardly discuss, however briefly, the history of London without mentioning the "revolution" of the Sixties: after decades of indifference London was once again the focus of world attention.

Fashion, music and rebellious youth took centre stage. The songs of the Beatles and the Rolling Stones swept away the traditional tear-jerking melodies; Mary Quant's mini-skirts were a scandal eventually adopted by the majority of women; hair was worn longer and Indian hemp began to sprout in London's flower pots. As a consequence of the adoption of English as the international *lingua franca*, hundreds of schools sprang up to

satisfy the demands of students from all four corners of the world, part and parcel of an unprecedented multiracial society and a remarkably profitable business that in spite of recent American competition continues to provide a significant boost to the British economy.

The whole of Great Britain has been affected by this particular boom, but London is the undisputed centre, the place to study for the 18-25 year-olds. In the late Seventies the hippies were replaced by the punks, a cult that has survived into the Nineties, and British youths either accepted the system or dropped out.

55 *Punks at Covent Garden. The punks are now an established part of the London landscape: the coloured crests, ripped and studded clothes and heavy make-up unite youngsters of different social origins but prevalently from the most impoverished and marginal classes. The "movement" that developed here in the Seventies spread throughout Europe; perhaps the last fashion trend to be exported from Great Britain.*

Today London is an immense city, a melting pot of languages, races, traditions and religions. A place where you can converse in English, but also in all the languages of the world, from Chinese to Italian. In its two- thousand-year history, London has expanded far beyond the confines of old Londinium and has become a crucible of races and myriad lifestyles. And this is its strength: thus we can all find and love our "own" personal London.

TRACES OF THE EMPIRE

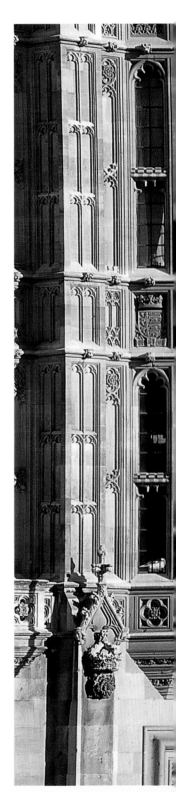

56 The complex structure of the Houses of Parliament is overlooked by the massive tower with four clock faces, erroneously thought of as Big Ben. The clock faces have a diameter of 7.5 metres and the copper minute hand is 4.25 metres long.

56-57 The simple, square-cut lines of the Palace of Westminster are decorated with spires and turrets, mullioned windows, statues and stone carvings. The building, home to the upper and lower houses, covers an area of around 4 hectares and contains 1,100 rooms and eleven courtyards. Along with meeting and debating rooms there are libraries, the offices of the politicians and their assistants and dining rooms. The interior is also characterised by typically Victorian the Gothic Revival opulence with carved wooden panelling, arched passageways and statues.

The choice of the point at which to start exploring a city is fundamental: the first impression may be so overwhelming as to inspire eternal love or implacable hatred for the place. This is especially true of London, a city that may be as green as Hyde Park or as dark as Victoria Station, as solemn as the Houses of Parliament or as turbulent as a painting by Turner, imperial or plebeian.

Some visitors, as soon as they reach the banks of the Thames, head straight off to pay their respects to the statue of Peter Pan in Kensington Gardens; others rush to the National Gallery. There are those incurable Sixties romantics who search Carnaby Street in vain for traces of Mary Quant and there are intellectuals who browse the bookshops of Charing Cross Road. There are the sophisticates who yearn after a Bond Street wardrobe and society wannabees who dream of meeting any of the members of the British royal family in spite of their recent trials and tribulations. We have decided to begin our tour with a museum that many miss, overshadowed as it is by numerous other temples of art and culture; a museum that also suffers from its location in that triumph of concrete in the Barbican Centre.

The Museum of London is, however, also in the heart of the City; that is to say in the very area in which London was born. From AD 43 when the Romans occupied the island, London and the City have been one and the same.

And while the subsequent phases of history, the great fires, the Luftwaffe bombing during the Second World War, may have erased all outward traces of the Roman city, the Museum of London exhibits what has been discovered over the course of the centuries and reconstructions of tragic or glorious temples: the statues that once graced a temple dedicated to Mithras, a Roman mosaic, the Cheapside workshops, the court of Elizabeth I.

In this museum you can witness the formation of a city, from *castrum* to trading hub to imperial capital and all this will help prepare you for the London of today.

57 top left The last rays of the setting sun disappear behind the Gothic Revival spires of the Houses of Parliament designed by the Victorian architect Sir Charles Barry.

57 top right The imposing Victoria Tower looms above the dark waters of the Thames.

The City, the area many associate with a lifeless agglomeration of banks and insurance houses, is in reality a self-contained miniature kingdom, with its own laws and hierarchies, a square mile with a population that at dusk falls from 350,000 to no more than 6,000. You will no longer see many gentlemen with regulation bowler hats and umbrellas, but increasing numbers of young climbers with the look of future millionaires. The moving spirit of the City is, however, still commerce; whether in shares or textiles it makes little difference. The Lord Mayor parades through his purely nominal realm once a year (in November) according to a ritual established in 1215 to pay homage to the head of the British magistrature with all the pomp and ceremony befitting an "almost absolute sovereign". The costumes, the carriages, the plumes of horses pass by the symbols of imperial power: law and finance.

The Law Courts, whilst not strictly belonging to the City — they are to be found on the eastern side of The Strand — are undoubtedly one of London's most characteristic sights. Bewigged, formal and apparently unchanged since the days of Queen Victoria, the British judges continue to administer the law. Not far from the civil courts, the Central Criminal Court, better known as the Old Bailey, rises where until the turn of the century was sited the celebrated

Newgate Prison, famous for the inhumane conditions in which prisoners were kept and immortalised by Dickens in his novels with a social theme. Around the Inns of Court you may meet judges and barristers with their famous wigs of white curls and the law students of Temple Inn who, according to an ancient tradition, are required to have dined at least 24 times at Inn's Hall before they are allowed to practise their chosen profession. You will also see Temple Bar, the memorial recording one of the eight gates that once gave access to the City and that is now its official, ceremonial entrance.

Beyond Fleet Street, the traditional home of British journalism, even though many of the newspapers have moved to cheaper parts of London, the names of the streets begin to remind us of the trades that for centuries dominated the area. Whilst in Cannon Street you may no longer be able to haggle over the price of wicks

60 left The Barbican
Centre replaced, in
1962, a series of
buildings demolished
by the German
bombing during the
Second World War.
The centre houses two
theatres, a concert
hall, cinemas, art
galleries, conference
and temporary
exhibition halls, a
library and the
Guildhall School of
Music.

60 top right A glass
of champagne
downed at the bar:
times really have
changed in the City.

for candles (Cannon being derived from candlestick), poultry or garlic, but the ancient Livery Companies, the craftsmens' and merchants' guilds, are still capable of exerting a certain influence over the administration of the City in spite of having lost a good deal of their original power. Some of the most sumptuous buildings in the City still belong to the surviving Livery Companies. Goldsmiths Hall for example, where precious metals are certified, is to be found in Foster Lane. It is in this corner of London that financial power is concentrated: the majestic facade of the Bank of England, the work of Sir John Soane, is an all but inviolable barrier to those lacking a valid reason for disturbing the "Old Lady of Threadneedle Street" as it has been called with a mixture of irony and affection since the days of Sir William Pitt. The young lions, the heirs to the traditional frock-coated bankers throng the area containing the bank, the Stock Exchange and the imposing, dramatic new headquarters of Lloyd's of London, the world's largest insurance group, celebrated for insuring anything against any risk, from ships to the shapely forms of leading ladies. Had it have been active in 1666 it would perhaps have insured the whole of London that in that year, early in September, was destroyed by the worst fire in its

history. The Monument, the tall Doric column designed by Sir Christopher Wren, the official architect of the London that rose out of the smoking ashes, is a memorial to a tragedy that, however grave in material terms, miraculously cost very few lives. Apparently, the height of the column is equal to the distance that separates it from the bakery in Pudding Lane where the fire broke out. From the summit of the Monument you can admire the panorama of the City, a constantly mutating view that takes in two buildings that inspire equal amounts of love and hate among Londoners.

It has to be admitted that the Barbican deserves a good deal of the abuse that is heaped upon it. Perhaps because there is too much concrete, something that as is well known the British have never liked. Perhaps because it took twenty years to build, or perhaps because it is so complex and labyrinthine that it takes an age to learn its layout. Or perhaps because it is a symbol of failure: failure to attract new inhabitants to the depopulated City; and failures are never popular. In any case the Barbican is nevertheless the place for lovers of classical theatre and music as it houses the Royal Shakespeare Company and the concert hall of the London Symphony Orchestra as well as restaurants, cinemas and cafés.

60-61 *The Royal Exchange faces onto a City square that also features two other symbols of the power invested in the Square Mile, the Bank of England and Mansion House, the official residence of the Lord Mayor. A curious fact is that the city's first public toilets were opened in front of the Royal Exchange in 1855.*

61 top *A view of the City. In this thicket of ultra-modern skyscrapers it is difficult to recognise the original nucleus of London that developed when London Bridge was still the only Thames crossing and the Roman walls still surrounded and protected the strategically important settlement.*

62 top left In 1092, the year of its inauguration, the White Tower was the tallest building in the city, its battlements reaching a height of 30 metres. Among the various treasures it contains of particular interest is St. John's chapel, built in stone specially imported from France.

62 top right The Beefeaters are members of the guard corps of the Tower of London. These forty-two volunteers have chosen to live and work on the site where William the Conqueror confirmed the Norman domination of the island.

62-63 Seen from above, the Tower of London complex is revealed in all its magnificence. The two turrets at the bottom right mark the main entrance; the large turret on the West Wall is the Beauchamp Tower that had the honour of housing illustrious prisoners. Behind the White Tower is the Jewel House where the Crown Jewels are kept.

63 top The Globe Royal, the golden orb (hollow inside but still weighing almost one and a half kilos) studded with gems and topped with a cross, is a symbol of the universal power of Christ. The double band of pearls that decorate it are set with rubies, emeralds and sapphires that are in turn surrounded by diamonds. The globe is used during the British sovereigns' coronation ceremony, together with the three swords of justice (representing mercy and spiritual and temporal justice) and the crossed sceptre set with one of the most fantastic diamonds of all time, the Great Star of Africa: 530 carats of pure light.

63 bottom The Imperial State Crown was created in 1837 for the coronation of Queen Victoria. Other crowns are also kept in the Tower of London, along with solid gold dinner services, antique weapons and ceremonial jewellery. These unique objects are quite literally priceless. The jewels of Elizabeth II's private collections were, on the other hand, valued a few years ago at 300 million pounds.

In contrast, love abounds where the Tower of London is concerned, a monument that every Londoner born within the sound of Bow Bells considers to be at least in part his very own. Nothing now remains of the original wooden edifice constructed by William the Conqueror in 1066 within the Roman city walls, but the White Tower from 1078 is still there, in the centre of a complex that has witnessed great episodes in British history. The legends associated with the site are myriad and there are ghosts by the dozen: Thomas Beckett, Anne Boleyn and Guy Fawkes walk the turrets and walls but have apparently very little effect on the impassable Yeoman Warders, the Tudor-costumed guards known as Beefeaters (because they once enjoyed a right to a daily ration of meat). The tower houses what can be considered as the oldest church in London, the Norman Chapel of St. John as well as some of the most interesting royal collections from that of ancient arms and armour to the fabulous Crown Jewels. The jewels mainly date from 1660, that is to say after the era of Cromwell who had melted down many of the earlier pieces. The diamonds as large as hens' eggs and the exotic jewellery can only be viewed from a distance and you cannot linger: a moving carpet whisks the crowds rapidly by otherwise they would remain entranced by the crown of the Prince of Wales, the royal sceptre with the Star of Africa diamond (530 carats), the Queen Mother's crown and the Koh-i-Noor, a "mountain of light" of 109 carats.

65 right Canary Wharf is the name of a commercial centre opened in Docklands a few years ago. It is dominated by the imposing Canada Tower, a 50-storey, 250-metre high skyscraper, designed by the American architect Cesar Pelli.

The Tower of London, that at one time marked both the centre and the boundary of the city, faces the opening Tower Bridge, the most famous of the bridges over the Thames and the last before the sea. The Gothic Revival architecture and the brilliant colour scheme of the bridge have made it a favourite subject for photographers and up until a few years ago it was also one of the sites of choice for aspiring suicides before the high walkways were closed in by glass panels. A short distance away, eastwards, extends the London dock area that has recently been subjected to a massive and radical restoration programme. Up until a few years ago the Isle of Dogs, the peninsula extending into the Thames, was a poor working class area with no prospects. Today it is the centre of a futuristic satellite town, a project that has aroused great controversy and has led to meteoric increases in house prices and the destruction of an entire community. The workers have given way to the yuppies who inhabit old warehouses transformed into luxurious homes and office blocks of steel and concrete. Even Prince Charles became involved in the controversy, making it clear that he did not like the idea of a forest of skyscrapers springing up alongside the docks. Nevertheless, the Canary Wharf tower is the tallest building in the city at 250 metres, an airport has been created on a tongue of land and some are already asking whether this is London or New York.

It is sufficient to turn West, following the Thames, to regain a sense of proportion. London Bridge, the oldest of the Thames crossings, appears in traditional songs and proverbs and has been here since Roman times. Various versions have been constructed in wood and then stone, been destroyed in fires, acted as the personal footbridge of

66 top left Despite
being an
unmistakable feature
of the building,
the two massive bell
towers of St. Paul's
Cathedral were not
part of the original
design by Sir
Christopher Wren.
The architect added

them later in 1707
and both were
designed to carry a
clock. The portico
also changed during
the construction
of the cathedral
as it was originally
designed with a single
row rather than
paired columns.

*66 bottom left St.
Paul's Cathedral has
been used for great
state ceremonies,
including the funeral
of Sir Winston
Churchill in 1965
and the marriage of
Lady Diana Spencer
and Prince Charles
in 1981.*

sovereigns and even, in 1967, sold brick by brick to an American company. Heading upstream along the Thames we find ourselves back in the City for one last courtesy call, this time on St. Paul's cathedral. The existing cathedral is actually the fifth church to be built on the site of a temple dedicated to Diana. It was designed by Sir Christopher Wren who, following the Great Fire of 1666, carefully eradicated all traces of the previous buildings — the last of which had been at least in part the work of Inigo Jones. Following the wooden and stone churches, a Saxon and then a Norman cathedral, monumental is the adjective that best describes Wren's St. Paul's with its 111-metre high dome, the Whispering Gallery that has delighted generations of visitors and the funerary monuments of great figures in British history. It may not be inviting to its congregation and may not inspire sudden conversions, but then Wren had quite different aims in mind. He wanted to erect a building that would stand as evidence of his genius over the centuries. The epitaph on his tomb — he was one of the first to be buried in the cathedral — leaves no doubt as to the opinion the architect had of himself: *Si monumentum requiris, circumspice* (If you seek a monument, look around you). The route from the City, following the course of the river, to the seats of contemporary power is equally monumental.

*66 top right The
mosaics on the ceiling
of the choir of St.
Paul's, a celebration
of gold-leaf and
brilliant colours,
were completed by
William Richmond
in 1890, long after
the opening of the
cathedral.*

*66 bottom right
This photo shows the
transept and the
choir of St. Paul's.
The cross-shaped plan
of the cathedral
ensures that all sight-
lines converge in the
centre under the
dome.*

*67 This photograph
shows the remarkable
dome of St. Paul's
from the inside. At
110 metres, the dome
is the world's second
largest after that of
St. Peter's in Rome.*

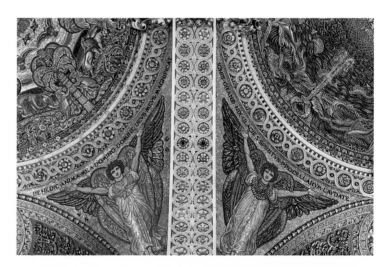

68 top Admiral Horatio Nelson continues to scan the horizon from his perch on the top of his column in the centre of Trafalgar Square. The column rises 50 metres, whilst the statue itself is 3 metres tall. The monument was completed in 1842 and it is said that prior to the installation of the statue, 14 builders gathered to eat supper on the top of the column.

68 bottom In the foreground can be seen one of the four bronze lions by Edward Landseer placed at the base of Nelson's Column. Thanks to its centrality and size, the square is today the site of choice for major demonstrations and each New Year's eve is celebrated here with rivers of beer and unseasonal dips in the fountains.

The Strand leads into Trafalgar Square, the site of mass protests and beer-fuelled New Year's Eve celebrations, the undisputed realm of tourists, pigeons and Horatio Nelson, the admiral who defeated the French fleet at the Battle of Trafalgar. The column on which his statue stands is 56 metres tall and the relief sculptures that decorate its base were cast from melted-down cannon from the ships defeated by the great British fleet. The tourists generally swarm in the direction of the National Gallery with its Neoclassical facade that dominates the immense square. A piece of advice? Given that entrance is free it would be better to subdivide your tour and come back more than once rather than risk overdosing on great art. Illustrious art historians frequently open lectures that are invaluable aids to understanding, but its is also pleasant to wander the galleries as the whim takes you. An afternoon dedicated to Rembrandt, a morning contemplating Monet, an entire day in front of the Leonardo cartoon, perhaps just an hour, but a profitable one, for the *Arnolfini Marriage* by Jan van Eyck.

68-69 Trafalgar Square is London's most important piazza; it was designed by John Nash and completed between 1830 and 1840. The occasion was the commemoration of Nelson's victory over the French fleet of Napoleon Bonaparte at Trafalgar in 1805. On the right can be seen the facade of St. Martin-in-the-Fields, an important church because it houses the remains of great artists and because it served as a model for the churches of the American colonies. Designed by James Gibbs early in the 18th century, the church today hosts recitals of church music.

70 top left The work
Noli me tangere *by
Titian, was hung in
the National Gallery
in 1856. The gallery
boasts a number of
works by the artist.*

70 top right The Woman
bathing in the stream
*is one of the best known
masterpieces
by Rembrandt and
is a portrait of his
companion Hendrickje*

*Stoffels. The inspiration
for the composition was
perhaps the biblical story
of Bethsheba. The work
was bequeathed to the
gallery by Reverend
Holwell Carr in 1831.*

70 bottom right
The Baptism of Christ
*was painted
by Piero della
Francesca for the
Priory of St. John the
Baptist at Sansepolcro.*

*It subsequently passed
through the hands
of various private
collectors and was
purchased by the
National Gallery
in 1861.*

70 bottom left The
National Gallery
also houses Young
Woman Standing at
a Virginal *by Jacob*

*van Vermeer that
came to the gallery
directly from the
antiques market in
1892.*

71 The Flemish
masters are well
represented in the
National Gallery. One
of the most famous
works is the Marriage

of Giovanni Arnolfini
and Giovanna
Cenami *by Jan Van
Eyck. The artist
himself can be seen
reflected in the convex*

*mirror on the wall in
the background,
immediately above
which is his signature.
The painting was
purchased in 1842.*

72-73 In 1870 Claude Monet stayed in London where he painted this view of the Thames and Westminster. He visited the National Gallery — where today some of his best known works are to be found — but he does not appear to have been particularly impressed.

72 top The Cornfield and cypress trees was painted by Vincent Van Gogh at Saint-Remy in 1889. It is part of the strong collection of modern art at the National Gallery.

72 bottom The Execution of the Emperor Maximillian was painted by Edouard Manet between 1867 and 1868. The influence of Goya can be seen.

73 *The* Dancer with castanets *is one of the most important works of the last phase of Pierre Auguste Renoir's career. This painting's companion piece,* Dancer with drum *is also in the National Gallery, both being purchased in 1961.*

Not far away, the National Portrait Gallery invites you to stroll among the characters that have made British history great. Almost next door, the church of St. Martin-in-the-Fields is the last resting place of illustrious artists — Hogarth, Reynolds and Chippendale — as well as being the parish church of Her Majesty the Queen. Elizabeth II herself lives at the end of avenue, beyond Admiralty Arch: the avenue in question is of course The Mall, also home to the Queen Mother who lives in Clarence House, whilst the arch itself recalls another sovereign, Queen Victoria, in whose memory it was constructed in 1910. Buckingham Palace, that today is more frequently cited in gossip columns than in political leaders, was designed by John Nash, and Queen Victoria was the first monarch to live there, to the great disapproval of the rest of the Royal family apparently. The 600 rooms of the palace, in spite of all the improvements that have been made over the years, are said to be remarkably uncomfortable. It should come as no surprise to learn that the Queen and Prince Philip actually live in relatively small apartments, reserving the State Rooms for ceremonial occasions. A few figures? The palace employs around 550 people in various service, management and maintenance roles. Among them are the curators of the Queen's art collections, a botanist, the keeper of the royal swans, the Queen's two ladies-in-waiting and a staff of 180 under the orders of the Master of the House (cooks,

75 This photo shows the members of the Royal Cavalry with their standards and banners. London remains a mecca for enthusiasts of military parades and ceremonies. There is the Ceremony of the Keys at the Tower of London, the Royal

Salutes in Hyde Park (on the occasion of royal birthdays), the Beating the Retreat ceremony at Horse Guards Parade and, once a year, the opening of Parliament during which the Queen travels from her official residence to Westminster.

76 top A number of motionless guards in line for the beginning of the most eagerly awaited ceremony of the year, Trooping the Colour.

76-77 The broad expanse of Horse Guards Parade houses part of the Trooping the Colour ceremony: the moment in which the Queen receives the salute from her soldiers. The various military corps parade in front of the sovereign before heading for Buckingham Palace. Horse Guards Parade also houses the offices of the Commander in Chief of the armed forces and here too there is a Changing of the Guard ceremony at 11 o'clock every morning.

77 top left This photo portrays the Queen on horseback with her guards. The Queen's love of horses is well known.

The Buckingham Palace stables, the Royal Mews, were designed by John Nash and are in part open to the public.

maids, confectioners and gardeners). How the daily life of the Palace is organised is not made public, even though recently a number of employees have foregone their prestigious but modest palace salaries in favour of the easy money offered by the tabloid press for tasty scoops. You can, on the other hand, watch the ceremony of the Changing of the Guard and visit the Queen's Gallery and the Royal Mews: the first houses part of the monarch's immense collection of art, the second some of the most beautiful historic carriages that on many official occasions are still preferred to the prestigious Rolls Royce limousines. Moreover, in order to raise the funds necessary for the reconstruction of Windsor Castle, devastated by fire, the Queen has for some time opened up certain parts of the palace to the public. There is no risk of bumping into Prince Charles, but you do get to see the Throne Room with its lavish velvets and gold stucco. Such an idea would never have occurred to the austere lady you meet in front of the palace: Queen Victoria, immortalised in an immense block of white marble, who reigned from 1837 to 1901, transforming in the process from the young girl depicted in a celebrated portrait by Franz Winterhalter to the opulent lady in widow's weeds, greedy and intransigent on questions of public and private morals and still capable at eighty years of age of rapping the knuckles of her son, the future King Edward VII, an impenitent womaniser.

77 right These photos show two further moments of the Trooping the Colour ceremony. The band of the infantry can be admired above with the Royal Cavalry. The stoicism of the members of the British guards corps is rightly famous: entire generations of tourists have provoked them, photographed them, adored them and searched for signs of enjoyment or irritation on their faces; always in vain, even though some claim that the latest recruits are more susceptible to flattering flashbulbs.

The Mall also features gates onto St. James's Park, the oldest of London's parks, created by Henry VIII and beloved of all his successors. Once a royal hunting reserve, the park is still one of London's most elegant green areas and is at its splendid best in spring. Swans, ducks and geese wait for crumbs on the lake, whilst music can often be heard from the small bandstand.

The typical harmony of English gardens can be found in nearby Green Park, an oasis of flowers and tranquility in the very heart of the city. This bucolic parenthesis introduces us to that part of London with the highest density of ministries. Whitehall also houses the Admiralty together with the offices of the head of M15, Her Majesty's counter espionage services. For some time now the post has been held by a woman — a sign of changing times.

Downing Street, home to the Prime Minister, is an almost anonymous city street. Up to just a few years ago, prior to the terrorist era, it was guarded by a lone policeman, armed with just a truncheon as a symbol of the fact that British democracy was part of the national heritage and political power had no reason to fear meeting its public.

The area also contains the Cabinet War Rooms, Banqueting House with its nine fabulous Rubens panels and, before reaching Parliament Square, a passage leading to New Scotland Yard that up to 1967 was the headquarters

of the London police force. You should also stop to see the Horse Guards who each day take part in the Changing of the Guard ceremony at Buckingham Palace. This is a favourite destination for tourists as they can admire not only the splendid animals — that some uncharitable gossips suggest Elizabeth II prefers to much of the human race — but also the imperturbability of the cavalrymen capable of remaining immobile even when assaulted by a thousand massed flash-guns.

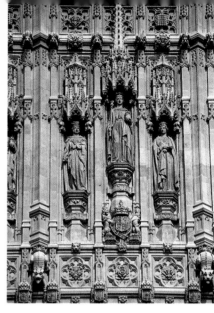

80 top The Palace of Westminster was a royal residence until Henry VIII, who preferred Whitehall Palace, came to the throne. Following its destruction in one of the numerous fires that have afflicted London over the centuries, it was rebuilt in the Gothic Revival style in the 19th century. Further modifications and additions were necessary after the Second World War. The Houses of Parliament were, in fact, badly damaged during the Blitz of 1940-41. In particular the House of Commons was rebuilt to the designs of Sir Giles Scott who copied the style preferred by Queen Victoria a hundred years earlier.

80-81 *This photograph shows the Palace of Westminster from the Thames. The transfer of the seat of power from the City, the original nucleus of London, to the current site took place in the 11th century. The only part of the medieval building remaining is Westminster Hall that dates back to 1097 and boasts a beamed ceiling from the 14th century.*

81 top *The clock-tower of the Palace of Westminster is 106 metres tall: at night the illuminated dials tell the time for the whole city. Over the years this has become one of the best known symbols of London and the sound of Big Ben, the 14-ton bell tolling the hours, is used to announce the programmes of the BBC, the state television and radio network. Inside the tower can be found the No. 1 Room in which at one time political agitators were locked. Among these was Emmeline Pankhurst, the ardent and combative English woman who early this century led the movement demanding the right to vote for women.*

81 bottom *Another photo of the Houses of Parliament. The public is allowed to witness the sittings at certain times of the day, whilst British citizens have a right to speak to the member of parliament they elected.*

Westminster is a veritable celebration of the Gothic and Gothic Revival styles. Parliament Square, created in the middle of the nineteenth century with the demolition of an area of miserable hovels, is inhabited by statues of great statesmen, and features the delicious little St. Margaret's Chapel, traditionally the parish church of the Members of the House of Commons, and, of course, Westminster Palace itself that many centuries ago was the residence of various monarchs and since 1547 the home of the British parliament. Little remains of the original building built in the eleventh century on the orders of William II, just Westminster Hall that, moreover, is closed to the public. And yet it was here that much of British history was played out. The rest of the building is in that eye-catching yet at the same time forbidding Gothic Revival style so dear to Queen Victoria and created by Charles Parry and Augustus Pugin in the mid-nineteenth century and restored after the destruction of the last World War. Then, of course, there is the clock tower. The chimes that during the last war announced the radio news broadcasts from the BBC, are those of Big Ben, the 14-ton bell cast in 1858 and installed by Sir Benjamin Hall from whom it takes its nickname. For lovers of the unusual, the tower contains the celebrated Number One room, the cell in which rabble rousers were detained. Here they tried to calm the overheat-

ed spirit of Emmeline Pankhurst, the famous suffragette. Ironically enough, in that same year, a monument was erected close by to another woman to have made political struggle her calling card: Boadicea, the Queen of the Iceni who defied the Roman conquerors.

At Westminster Abbey the Gothic architecture is authentic and here you really do get an impression of history. Over nine centuries have passed since Edward the Confessor gave orders for its construction to begin on the site of an earlier Benedictine monastery. The good king had little time to benefit from his actions, dying just a week after the consecration of the abbey late in 1065.

82 top left This long row of coats of arms outside Westminster Abbey shows the extent to which the building has been linked with the history of the English Crown. From the times of Elizabeth I, Westminster Abbey has in fact been an independent body answering directly to the sovereign.

82 top right A statue of Oliver Cromwell in Westminster Abbey. A member of the minor provincial nobility, Cromwell the politician became the leading figure in the events that led to the execution of Charles I.

However, Edward was the first monarch to be buried at Westminster, and subsequently the Abbey has become the traditional site for coronations and royal burials. The building we see today actually dates from the second half of the thirteenth century. Further modifications were made later, whilst the interior, in keeping with eighteenth-century tastes, was filled with funerary monuments to great poets, from Chaucer to Ben Jonson (buried standing upright) and Tennyson. Plaques have been erected to commemorate others such as Shakespeare, Shelley, Keats, T. S. Eliot and last, but by no means least, Oscar Wilde. Those who want a review of the major or minor figures in British history are faced with an embarrassment of riches: you may come across David Livingstone and Gladstone, Issac Newton and Jonas Hanway, the first Londoner to use an umbrella, Elizabeth I and Bloody Mary, Mary Stuart and Henry VII. Westminster Abbey is a "Royal Peculiar" as it comes under a special jurisdiction and is directly controlled by the Crown. There are those who say it is a celebration of death in its most solemn form, but it is certainly the London monument that best reflects the history of the realm.

84 top The stained-glass chapel windows colour the interior of Westminster Abbey. The Abbey is especially famous for the number of illustrious figures buried there, and in fact much of British history is united under its roof. The celebrated Poets' Corner was "inaugurated" with the erection of a memorial tomb to Geoffrey Chaucer in 1556, over a century after his death. Ben Jonson was buried, according to his express wishes, standing upright, whilst other great writers from Shakespeare to Keats, from Kipling to Oscar Wilde are commemorated with plaques or sumptuous funerary monuments. Many political figures have also had the honour of being buried here: Gladstone, Chamberlain and Attlee for example. The remains of Oliver Cromwell, on the other hand, had a troubled history; buried in the Abbey, they were then exhumed during the period of the restoration.

84-85 The central nave of the Abbey is about 10 metres wide but more than 30 metres high. This lends the building a very accentuated verticality. In the background can be seen the screen separating the choir and the sanctuary. The Abbey also contains a splendid cloister with the Undercroft Museum housing a collection of effigies and sacred objects, and Westminster School, a prestigious private academy founded by Elizabeth I following the closure of the schools run by the religious orders.

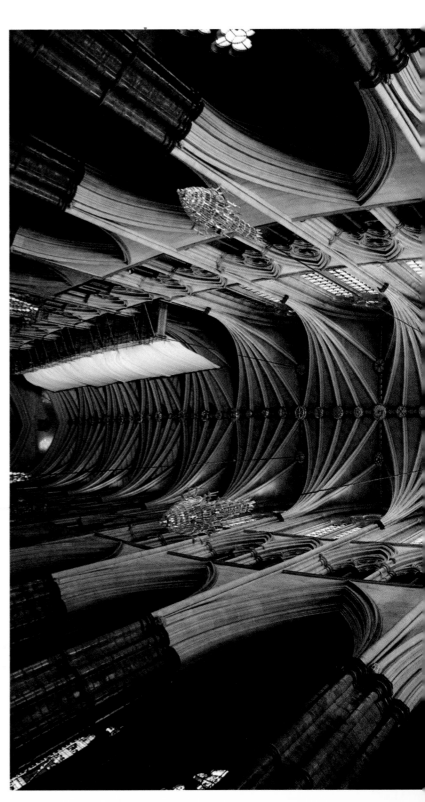

84 bottom Another of the stained-glass windows of Westminster Abbey that also contains the Grave of the Unknown Soldier, with a memorial stone to Sir Winston Churchill nearby, and the Warriors' Chapel dedicated to the victims of all wars in all ages.

85 top The choir contains the chapel of Edward the Confessor with his shrine, his throne and, until recently, the Stone of Scone on which the Scottish sovereigns were crowned.

86-87 Westminster Cathedral is the most important Catholic church in London. It was built on the site of a prison at the end of the 19th century, being completed in 1903, to the designs of John Francis Bentley. The architectural style, an unusual blend of Byzantine and Renaissance, is accentuated by the external finish in red brick and white stripes of Portland stone. The bell-tower is 87 metres tall and contrasts strongly with the Gothic architecture of the nearby Westminster Abbey. An earlier project featured a Gothic Revival style church but this was abandoned as being too expensive. The cathedral is dedicated to the Precious Blood of Our Lord Jesus Christ.

86 top and 87 The interior of Westminster Cathedral is a triumph of marble. It has been calculated that it contains over 100 different types from all over the world. The Byzantine influence is seen in the nave with its enormous green marble columns that recall those in the church of Santa Sophia in Istanbul.

The building was commissioned by Cardinal Henry Edward Manning who intended it to be a memorial to Nicholas Patrick Wiseman, the first Archbishop of the Catholic Church of England following the Anglican Reformation under Henry VIII. Among the works of art in the cathedral are the magnificent reliefs of the Stations of the Cross created by Eric Gill during the First World War and a sculpture by Giacomo Manzù. The organ is also considered to be an authentic masterpiece. The fine acoustics of the cathedral have led to its becoming a summer concert hall that is very popular with enthusiasts of sacred and classical music.

89 *The collection of works by Turner (shown in the photo is "Crossing the Brook") is housed in the Clore Gallery, a new wing of the Tate Gallery. Such is the importance and size of the collection, that the curators are obliged to exhibit the paintings and sculptures in rotation. Students and academics are permitted to visit the stores and admire the masterpieces that are waiting their turn to be placed in the public galleries.*

Before leaving this part of London you must press on as far as the Tate Gallery which is virtually on the banks of the Thames.

It was Sir Henry Tate, the philanthropist sugar tycoon, who financed this art gallery originally destined to house only British contemporary art but which has instead become a mecca for lovers of contemporary art in general. In the future, part of the collection will be transferred to the restored Bankside Power Station. For now, you should make every effort to visit the Clore Gallery, a wing added to the main body of the Tate that contains the extraordinary paintings of William Turner, triumphs of light and raging elements.

88 top *The portico of the main entrance to the Tate Gallery faces the Thames: the gallery was constructed thanks to the patronage of Sir Henry Tate, the sugar magnate.*

88 centre *One of the Neo-Classical rooms leads into one of the world's most important collections of modern art. According to the intentions of the Tate Gallery's benefactor, it was to hold collections of exclusively British art, but subsequently the acquisitions policy was extended to include the most significant representatives of international painting and sculpture.*

88 bottom *A visit to the Tate Gallery is a unique experience, not only for the quality of the works of art on show, but also for the way in which they are presented.*

90 *The interior of the Victoria and Albert Museum in the heart of South Kensington, reflects the tastes of the period in which it was constructed. The fusion of influences ranging from Gothic to the Renaissance houses one of the broadest collections in the capital: from ceramics to textiles, from silverware to figurative art. The most important collection, however, is that of the engravings and drawings in the Henry Cole wing. The Print Room houses some 50,000 works.*

90-91 *The great Albert Hall "pancake" conceals an important concert hall. This building is dedicated to the Prince Consort and the Greek-style friezes depict the triumphs of the arts and science. Prince Albert was, in fact, distinguished by his patronage and his enthusiasm for the wonders of modern technology.*

91 top left *At Queen Victoria's behest, a memorial was erected in 1876 to her beloved consort Prince Albert who had died 15 years earlier. The structure is dedicated not only to the Prince himself, but also to his great passion for scientific progress. The whole was completed in that Gothic Revival style that so appealed to the Queen and that characterizes the "Museum Quarter".*

We find museum after museum, as we move away from the Thames in the direction of one of London's green lungs, Hyde Park. The Kensington district is particularly devoted to Queen Victoria and her beloved consort Albert, commemorated at Kensington Gardens by the Albert Memorial, a bizarre Gothic Revival folly, a paean to unrestrained kitsch. In front of the memorial stands another building constructed at the behest of Queen Victoria, the Royal Albert Hall: whilst not blessed with exceptional acoustics, it is nevertheless a symbol of the era in which it was built. Certain distinguished Londoners continue to frequent the concert hall, enjoying a privilege that dates back more than a hundred years and that is destined to endure: in 1863 whosoever decided to contribute £100 to the financing of the building project obtained the right of admission to the concerts for themselves and their heirs for 999 years. This says much about the excellent opinion that the Victorian architects had of themselves and the durability of their work!

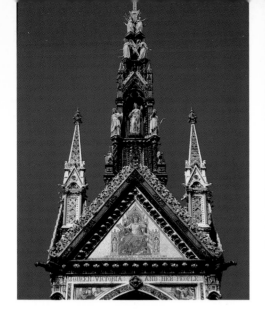

91 top right
The skeleton of the Diploducus *dinosaur* that welcomes visitors in the entrance hall of the Natural History Museum in South Kensington attracts not only children but also thousands of adults fascinated by a bygone world.
The museum was built in the high Victorian period - 1881 - by Alfred Waterhouse, using the most modern techniques. The enormous halls allowed visitors to take an extraordinary trip through the wonders of nature: the museum is a veritable citadel of science that includes an extensive geological section and an exceptional botanical reference collection containing dried leaves of all the known plants.

The group of museums located in South Kensington makes the area a target for academics but also for children. Taking a child to the Natural History Museum, for example, can be great fun.

The gigantic dinosaur stretching its neck out along the immense gallery introduces a journey back through time to an era 65 million years ago, whilst the hall in which the effects of an earthquake are simulated unleashes cries of wonder and terror.

Close by, the Science Museum's interactive games bring even the youngest children into contact with the worlds of technology and physics.

The Victoria and Albert Museum is, on the other hand, perhaps more suitable for adults. Officially the museum was created to display examples of "fine and applied arts", a rather broad agenda that is reflected by the variety of artefacts to be found in around twelve kilometres of halls and galleries.

It is, of course, impossible to see everything, but how could you pass over the Constable collection, the Raphael cartoons, the fashion gallery, the furniture, the art of the goldsmiths or the Indian art? Equipped with a letter of introduction confirming their academic good standing, anybody can use the library and handle rare manuscripts and drawings by celebrated artists, taking a plunge into the past. One of the most important characteristics of the Victoria and Albert Museum as it is known is that there is something of interest for everybody, from the engagement ring of a Berber princess to the embroidered cushion of an abbess, from Donatello to an obscure Celtic craftsman.

93 top There is touch of Jane Eyre in this painting by Richard Redgrave, The Governess.
It probably depicts the life of a young woman employed by a wealthy London family of the 19th century: an endless sequence of identical days without even the consolation of an attractive Mr Rochester appearing on the horizon.

Having left the museums your thirst for greenery and nature can easily be satisfied by entering Kensington Gardens, a very fashionable park in the reign of George II from which you may catch a glimpse of one of the members of the royal family who live in Kensington Palace. Some of the rooms of the palace are open to the public and you can visit the Orangery, the beautiful conservatory for citrus fruit trees built for Queen Anne early in the eighteenth century. Children, and those adults who still remember their childhood, will not want to miss seeing Peter Pan; his statue, sculpted by Sir George Frampton in 1912, is a must for those nostalgic for bygone times. The children who at the turn of the century played with their hoops and sailed model boats on the Serpentine, the lake that unites Kensington Gardens with Hyde Park, inspired James Matthew Barrie to create the legendary character who decided never to grow up. Children continue to play on the perfect lawns and amongst the great trees in the gardens, as they do in Hyde Park, which like all the major London parks was once a royal hunting reserve. This is commemorated in the Rotten Row bridle-path linking St. James's with Kensington Palace

(the unusual name derives from the French phrase *route du roi*). Here each morning you can see the guards of the Household Cavalry heading towards Buckingham Palace, part of a long-established ritual. Sunday mornings should naturally be passed at Speaker's Corner at the northeast tip of the park, near Marble Arch, where anybody can express their views be they doomsday preachers, political activists or entertainers. The speakers attract crowds of onlookers and there are frequently true debates.

Beyond Marble Arch, built in Serravezza Italian marble and once located in front of Buckingham Palace, you find yourself walking down Baker Street immortalised by Sir Arthur Conan Doyle whose hero Sherlock Holmes resided at number 221 B. The fact that the writer deliberately chose a non-existent address has never discouraged fans of the great detective for whom a museum has been created in which they can immerse themselves in the Victorian atmosphere in which Holmes and Doctor Watson worked to outwit the forces of crime. Whilst it is of course a thorough sham, it is all so realistic that even the sharpest of observers will be taken in by the curved pipe, the deerstalker and the magnifying glass.

96 top *Victoria Tower Gardens, wedged in between the Thames, Millbank, and the Houses of Parliament (that can be seen in the photo), represent an oasis of peace and quiet in the pulsing heart of the metropolis.*

At the far end of Baker Street lies another of London's jewels, Regent's Park. The greenery of the lawns and trees is in sharp contrast with the blinding white of the Regency buildings designed by John Nash. The work of this architect is to be found in various parts of London such as Carlton House Terrace along the Mall, but the idea of a city park could, at least in part, only be realised thanks to the megalomania of George, the Prince of Wales and regent in place of his father George III of Hanover from 1811 to 1820. The prince was no saint, but he was not insensitive to the appeal of the arts and the idea of his name being linked with a style was very attractive. With his protection and money, Nash managed to complete in just a few years the extraordinary Sussex Terrace with its Corinthian capitals, the monumental Chester Terrace with a Doric facade and a Renaissance-style courtyard, Cumberland Terrace. The whole complex was erected within what was once one of Henry VIII's hunting estates, a park that also houses London Zoo and, during the summer, the performances of the Royal Shakespeare Company.

96-97 Hyde Park is to be found to the east of Kensington Gardens, from which it is separated by the West Carriage Drive running from Alexandra Gate to Victoria Gate. The magnificent emerald green lawns make

the park one of the Londoners' favourite haunts and they come here to walk their dogs or perhaps to eat a picnic lunch. Hyde Park was also once a royal hunting estate; it was James I who opened it to the public.

97 top Thanks to a law passed in 1872, anybody who has something to say can say it in the northwest corner of Hyde Park. Thus was created Speakers' Corner, the platform of choice for all kinds

of dreamers and idealists, inventors and revolutionaries, religious fanatics and materialists. It should perhaps be remembered that at one time public hangings were held here.

97 centre St. James's Park is without doubt one of the capital's most attractive green areas. From here your gaze may range from the severe Gothic Revival architecture of the Houses of Parliament (to the right) to the twin spires of Westiminster Abbey (centre).

97 bottom Rotten Row is a bridle path in spite of its curious name that hardly invites one to go for a ride. It derives from the French route du roi as this was the road that linked St. James's with Kensington Palace in which William III had decided to live.

98 top There is a real sense of history in the British Museum. The British Library houses the illuminated gospels of the Bishop of Lindisfarne from 698, two of the four existing copies of the Magna Carta Libertatum, the "constitution" conceded by King John Lackland in the 13th century, the Gutenberg Bible, manuscripts and ancient maps of the world.

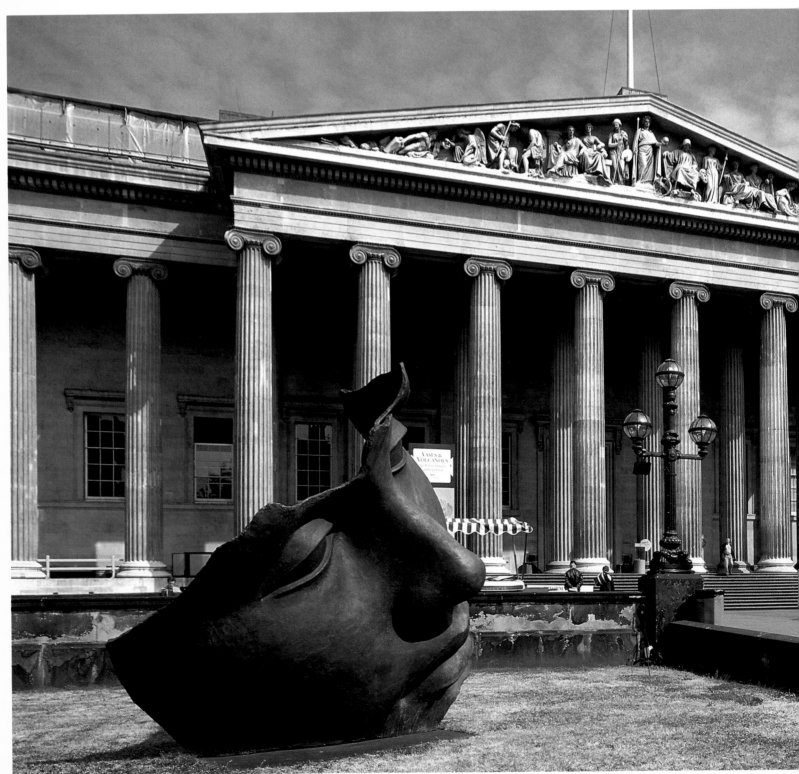

A very different atmosphere is to be found further north. Virginia Woolf and the British Museum are two symbols of Bloomsbury, once so elegant as to be closed off with gates keeping out the hoi polloi, but the subject of alternate fortunes.

The discreet streets and contrasting spacious squares of the area became early this century the home of the Bloomsbury Group, an informal set of writers, academics and artists who lived and worked side by side. Virginia and Leonard Woolf, Edward Morgan Forster, Roger Fry, Lytton Strachey and Clive Bell were following in the footsteps of other intellectuals who in the past had been attracted to the area by the presence of the British Museum, officially opened to the public in 1759 at Montague House, and by the University of London and the numerous bookshops.

The British Museum today houses one of the world's greatest collections, and climbing the steps to the entrance of the current Neoclassical building built in the middle of the nineteenth century by Robert Smirke signifies coming into contact with such a wealth of relics and artefacts as to set your head spinning.

Most visitors tour the halls and corridors in a kind of bemused trance, stopping perhaps in front of the Rosetta Stone, the key to our understanding of hieroglyphs, the so-called Elgin Marbles from the Parthenon, or the Sumerian, Assyrian and Babylonian treasures.

However the medieval, oriental and numismatic sections are no less fascinating, and true scholars can make use of the grandiose Reading Room, a dome-topped circular hall that has accommodated the most illustrious figures in the realms of political thought, art and literature.

The Egyptian section of the British Museum was part of the original bequest by Sir Hans Sloane. However, it was only after the surrender of the French army in Egypt in 1801, that the sculptures in Hall 25 began to reach London.

101 top The Rosetta Stone is probably the most famous exhibit in the museum. This slab of basalt found by a group of French soldiers during the Napoleonic expedition of 1799 is inscribed with a text in three languages: hieroglyphics, demotic and Greek. In 1822 the scholar Champollion finally completed the deciphering of the text and opened the way to an understanding of hieroglyphics.

101 centre The great Hunts of Ashurbanipal, bas-relief friezes in alabaster, date back

to 600 BC and once decorated the interior of the Assyrian king's palace at Nineveh. These were found in 1854 and immediately transferred to the British Museum.

101 bottom The celebrated bust of Rameses II, today exhibited in the Egyptian Hall of the British Museum, was brought to England by Giovan Battista Belzoni.

102 top *The elegant Russell Hotel, facing onto the square of the same name, was opened in 1900. Finished in red terracotta, the hotel conserves a very attractive Victorian atmosphere veiled with a sense of nostalgia for times past.*

102-103 *Somerset House is a grandiose complex in the Neo-Classical style designed by William Chambers in the second half of the 18th century. On one side it faces on to the Thames and on the other the Strand. The building houses the Courtauld Institute, a small but sophisticated portrait gallery noted for its Impressionist and Post-Impressionist masterpieces.*

103 top *Charing Cross Road is a name well known to bibliophiles: the best antiquarian booksellers in London and probably in the world are to be found here. Even for novices it is a pleasure to browse amongst the antique and precious volumes, fragrant with the dust of history. As well as antiquarian bookshops, central London is well served by many high quality bookshops, such as Hatchards in Piccadilly (top right).*

102 bottom *The atmosphere of Soho is a different kettle of fish. Here composed dignity is replaced by a desire for entertainment and excess.*

Covent Garden could hardly be overlooked on even a brief tour of London: the ancient kitchen garden of Westminster Abbey and transformed in the mid-seventeenth century, the area has become something of a symbol of the city. Who is to say whether the Duke of Bedford, when in 1630 he set about creating an Italian-style piazza surrounded by porticoes, could have had any idea of the success of his project in the centuries to come? Very little remains of the original structure but Covent Garden is one of the focal points of London's social life. On one side stands the Royal Opera House and where once were to be found the city's wholesale fruit, vegetable and flower markets today there is a plethora of stalls, shops and boutiques and the complex is famed for its street entertainers. Many of them perform in front of the church of St. Paul, designed by Inigo Jones and known as the actors' (theatrical rather than cinematic) church.

Another side of show business is a characteristic of Soho in the heart of the West End. In the not so distant past, Soho was synonymous with vice and depravation. Even the least worldly of tourists had heard of the side streets and small squares in which you could find more or less anything from ladies of easy virtue to porn shops, from fringe theatres to shops specialising in cinematic memorabilia. Four centuries ago this was open countryside, and the very name of the district apparently derives from a hunting cry. Immigrants, especially French refugees from religious persecution, began to build houses and workshops and in time the area began to attract the most unconventional of artists from Mozart to Verlaine, from Oscar Wilde to Dylan Thomas. Following the thorough "disinfestation" of the area demanded by a number of inhabitants, Soho now appears much more respectable, many of the more dubious clubs have disappeared and you can now safely browse the bookshops and exotic grocery stores. Bibliophiles head for Charing Cross Road where there are countless specialist antiquarian and art bookshops. The miles of dusty shelves are capable of providing you with that particularly rare volume, an unusual title that happens to take your fancy for just a few pounds, an autographed first edition or precious manuscripts. As the evening draws on all that remains is to choose one of one of the many West End theatres, one of the cinemas in and around Leicester Square or perhaps one of the myriad Indian, Italian or Chinese restaurants that line Old Compton Street.

104 top Mayfair, a Georgian district considered to be among the most exclusive in London, boasts elegant residential buildings such as those facing onto Berkeley Square.

Mayfair is a very different matter. It has been synonymous with wealth, power and unmistakably British class since the eighteenth century when the area between Piccadilly, Oxford Street, Regent Street and Park Lane became the fashionable quarter par excellence. The white facade of Regent Street was designed by John Nash for the Prince Regent and was intended to unite Regent's Park and Carlton House, the royal residence. Wide, crowded, elegant and opulent, with its luxury shops and restaurants such as Garrards, the Queen's jeweller charged with the maintenance of the Crown Jewels, and the Café Royal, frequented from the end of the nineteenth century by all the city's most successful artists and still very much a place to be seen, Regent Street leads on to Bond Street, Jermyn Street and Burlington Arcade. That is to say paradise for sophisticates and snobs who can buy their hats, shirts and umbrellas from the same shops that serve Prince Philip and Prince Charles, or have their hair cut by the same stylist as Princess Diana. The less frivolous may prefer to visit the Museum of Mankind that contains the ethnographic collection of the British Museum, or the Royal Academy to catch up on the latest trends in contemporary art. However, we are now heading in the direction of Piccadilly Circus and there is not a museum or park that can stop us: sooner or later everybody gets there. There is no escaping, and it is hard to say what is the attraction of this cherub and his arrows. In actual fact the statue is not of Eros as everybody presumes, but of the very Victorian Angel of Christian Charity. It is said that his arrows indicate the location of the site where at the time of Elizabeth I stood a famous brothel. And in fact peccadilloes continue to be committed in the surrounding pubs and clubs and even on the street corners. There are those who choose this cross-roads from which to begin their exploration of London. It may not be the centre of the universe but it certainly makes a great starting point.

105 Regent Street was designed by John Nash early in the 19th century to allow the Prince Regent easy access to Regent's Park from Carlton House. The road begins at Waterloo Place where it takes the name Lower Regent Street (in the photo) and cuts diagonally through the centre of the city.

106 The navel of the world is how Londoners think of Piccadilly Circus. At the very centre of the centre of the universe is the statue of Eros shooting his arrow. The small statue was erected in 1892 in memory of the Earl of Shaftesbury and actually represents the Angel of Christian Charity.

In Elizabethan times the area had a rather unsavoury reputation thanks to a very popular brothel, Piccadilla House. It must have been a very fashionable locale if it gave its name not only to the surrounding area but also to an Elizabethan delicacy, the pickadil.

In the late 20th century the principal characteristic of Piccadilly Circus would appear to be the huge neon signs advertising fast food chains and electronics giants. And whilst to the southeast lies the elegant St. James's area, to the northwest is Soho, London's peccadillo-quarter par excellence.

107-110 London at dusk, as seen from the former County Hall facing onto the Thames a few yards from Westminster Bridge. In the background can be seen the tower housing Big Ben and the Houses of Parliament.

111 The Haymarket, in the very heart of London, links Piccadilly Circus with Pall Mall. The incessant traffic, the lights and the crowds provide unequivocal evidence that this street is one of the focal points of the West End. It features the Theatre Royal, embellished with a John Nash portico (to the left in the photo), and the Guinness World of Records, a museum devoted to incredible facts and figures of all kinds.

*114 top left
This photo shows
some of the carts that
are used annually
on the occasion of the
Parade of Beer
Transport, a lively
demonstration
of bygone means
of transport.*

*114 top right The
London bobbies are
a true institution:
"armed" only with a
truncheon, a whistle
and a pair of
handcuffs, they seem
more akin to
courteous and
accommodating PR
men than police
officers and make
a valuable
contribution to the
image of their city.*

*114-115 The Mall,
the triumphant
avenue leading to
Buckingham Palace,
was created when the
facade of the royal
residence was rebuilt.
In the background can
be seen the monument
erected in memory of*

*Queen Victoria in
1911. The avenue is
particularly lively
during ceremonial
occasions in which the
Queen is taking part
and she glides past in
one of her sumptuous
carriages or exclusive
limousines.*

*115 top Not all of
the city can boast
monuments and
works of art, but even
in the most obscure
corners of London
you can always rely
on a passing black
cab to remind you
where you are.*

London Transport is keen to point out in its information leaflets that all their buses still carry the same logo; this does nothing of course to soften the blow. Similarly those tourists completing a pilgrimage to Carnaby Street in the hope of finding something of the spirit of Swinging London will probably break down in tears when faced with yet another shop selling T-shirts identical to those they could find at home.

But all is not lost. Thankfully London is so large and variegated as to allow one and all to find their own perfect niche. Perhaps not on your first day or even in your first week, but sooner or later it will happen. And in that instant it is a case of unconditional love that will allow you to forget the rush hour crowds on the tube, the omnipresent hamburgers of the fast food joints and the interminable queues for theatre tickets.

It has happened to me on more than one occasion. The first was when I was standing in front of Monet's water lilies one summer's day. An illustrious art historian was giving a lunch-time lecture on the enormous painting hanging in the National Gallery. I was immediately seized with an irresistible desire to see flowers, trees and lawns and hurried to the nearest park, St. James's. And there I was enchanted: this was "home". The royal swans were simply disguised geese as in the story of Mary Poppins (the real story not the adulterated Disneyesque version) when the Keeper of the Pigs imagines himself in the role of a prince and the Keeper of the Geese in that of a princess. And then there was Bloomsbury, the writers' quarter, or at least it was at one time. If they ever get round to inventing a time machine perhaps the best era to live in London would be early in the twentieth century when as well as Virginia Woolf, the area housed critics and patrons like Roger Fry, Americans in search of fortune like Ezra Pound, luckless artists, idealists and suffragettes. The pilgrimage is obligatory for lovers of literature: you could spend hours flicking through the latest publications or browsing amongst the second-hand books in Dillons, the immense bookshop facing onto Gower Street at the foot of an unusual and beautiful Gothic Revival building. According to Thackeray, Russell Square was home to the two friend and foe families, the Osbornes and the Sedleys, whilst Dickens lived in Doughty Street not far from Macklenborough Square where Virginia Woolf committed suicide in 1941. Need I add that these are some of my favourite authors?

Another indelible memory concerns the long afternoons spent in the National Art Library of the Victoria and Albert Museum, consulting precious manuscripts.

In any Italian library the bureaucratic rigmarole involved in obtaining a

*115 bottom Carnaby
Street is just a minor
road between Oxford
Street and Regent
Street, but during the
Sixties it became the
symbol of Swinging
London: even the
austere Oxford
English Dictionary
identified it with
youthful,
extravagant clothing.
Thirty years later it
has undeniably
declined: it is now
merely a chaotic
succession of shops
selling identical tatty
souvenirs and clothes.
However, there are
many nostalgic fifty-
somethings who still
visit out of respect for
the good old days.*

reading permit would have been interminable. Here, on presentation of a letter of introduction from an unknown — to them — Venice university lecturer, a pass was sent to my home address that allowed me to consult all the documents I wanted to. Biros, scissors and chewing gum were naturally forbidden but pencils were fine.

Other travellers could recount different experiences, those moments in which London fever took an unbreakable grip. Some remember with gratitude the solicitude of the bobbies, the London policemen armed only with truncheons and a severe yet paternal expression.

An aged Milanese lady told me of how she lost herself in the labyrinthine city before being literally "picked up" by a gigantic bobby who kindly deposited her on the right bus, told her how many stops to count and calculated the correct fare. A few minutes later she was in front of her hotel.

The Metropolitan Police force is a British institution as deeply rooted as afternoon tea and cucumber sandwiches. They have no right to strike, they do not earn very much and frequently they are obliged to tackle complex situations; and yet being a member of the force, created way back in 1829, is still an honour and recompense is to be found in the gratitude of the Londoners and the tourists who look upon the bobby as a kind of elder brother.

Dedicated theatre-goers get a thrill just reading a list of the London theatres with around forty in the central area alone and another sixty further out in the suburbs (but still well served by the public transport network). From the great musicals to the most classical of Shakespearean productions, from major West End shows to those of the most alternative companies, the choice is infinite. But then the British are a very "theatrical" people as the queues at the box offices demonstrate.

Agatha Christie's *The Mousetrap* has been playing continuously since 1952. Every evening in theatreland, as the area of the West End with the greatest concentration of theatres is known, curtains rise on the musicals of Andrew Lloyd Webber or the sophisticated comedies of Noel Coward, on the light operas of Gilbert and Sulllivan and Shakespearean tragedies.

The theatre with the capital "T" however is the National Theatre that is actually to be found on the "wrong" side of the river, the South Bank, rather than in the West End. Its first director, Laurence Olivier, immediately made his own classical mark, but today the National also puts on experimental works and has introduced some of the new stars of British drama such as Peter Shaffer.

Another factor that attracts people to London, at least those able to afford it, is shopping. Whilst it is often said that major stores are to be found everywhere and everything can be bought anywhere, only Harrods can boast the motto *Omnia omnibus ubique*: all things for all people, everywhere. Opened in 1849 by Henry Charles Harrod, and now owned by Egyptian financiers, the great department store is as British as you could possibly hope.

If you do not want to buy anything, neither hat-pins nor elephants (should you so desire it could be arranged) you can simply visit some of the departments as if they were museums. The Food Hall, for example, that at Christmas is full of hampers filled with every imaginable delicacy; the household goods department with table settings worthy of an emperor; the musical instrument department where you can usually count on an improvised concert as potential clients try out the goods. And, for the ladies, if you will pardon the indelicacy, the toilets.

The Queen does her Christmas shopping here and if after hours you see a Rolls Royce drawing up at a discreet back door it may well be her, the sovereign in person, arriving to choose a gift for a friend.

Another institution for Londoners, and especially for bargain-hunting visitors, are the various bric-a-brac, junk and modern antique markets. Those in the know say that Portobello is now the best place to practice your Italian: every Saturday the market is overrun with tourists and what does it matter if the porcelain is chipped, the glassware unmatched and the teapots stained? A little of the cockney spirit is still to be found in some of the perhaps less well known markets in Camden Town and Petticoat Lane. On the other hand, at Brick Lane in the East End, or in Brixton, the atmosphere is decidedly exotic. If there is still anybody who refuses to believe in the cosmopolitan nature of modern London then they should visit these two markets.

The first is an Indian enclave, the second a little part of the Caribbean: at least something good came out colonialism, bringing all the colours and exotic aromas of distant lands to the grey imperial capital. Halfway between an open air theatre and a bazaar you can find anything and everything at Covent Garden, a sight not to be missed, as being perfectly placed in the city centre, it makes an ideal resting place between one monument and the next.

The numerous stalls and small shops include one on the lower level selling perfect, ever-so English dolls' houses, complete, right down to the miniature silk roses to set in George III silver vases on an inlaid sideboard. Other destinations capable of triggering London fever? One might be Kew Gardens, the Royal Botanical Gardens. This is just the place to understand why the British consider their countryside to be a park without rubbish bins. The greenhouses, now restored to their original splendour following the hurricane that devastated the South of the country, contain the world's greatest collection of orchids — one even Nero Wolf would be proud of — and recently saw the blooming of a huge tropical flower, the titan, ugly and foul-smelling but so rare as to attract thousands of visitors eager to photograph it. The herbarium contains 6 million examples and 40,000 plants grow in the greenhouses and gardens. Kew Gardens is just one of the many parks that can be visited but thanks to some strange enchantment it exerts a greater attraction than the others, an attraction almost as intense as the sensation of finding yourself immersed in perfectly constructed yet thoroughly respected nature.

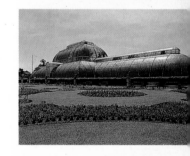

121 bottom The Palm
House in Kew Gardens,
designed in 1840 by
Decimus Burton, has
recently been completely
restored. The Royal
Botanical Gardens,
located in the London
suburbs, were founded
by Princess Augusta in
1759 and are renowned
for their magnificent
greenhouses.

Last but not least there are the pubs. In order to capture the traditional atmosphere you need to find a pub similar to the one described by P. G. Wodehouse in the Mulliner story in which the regulars knew each other not by name but by what they drank. Or go back to the days in which ladies were not even admitted to these temples of male bonding. Visiting London's oldest pub, the Prospect of Whitby — in the Docklands area — is not much help.

At one time it was a rough den of adventurers, smugglers, thieves and wrongdoers worthy of John Gay's *The Beggar's Opera*, but is now a chic bar in which the suits of the new East End development area drink champagne and eat lunch with a view of the Thames. There are of course a few ghosts, but those you will find throughout London. The best strate-

124 right
The George Inn at Southwark is perhaps the most celebrated pub in London. It was built in the medieval style in 1676 and its historical value has led

to its acquisition by the National Trust. It is the city's only old pub to be equipped with a gallery and at one time was also used as an open-air theatre.

gy, therefore, is choose a pub at random, maybe one off the beaten tourist track and claim it as your own.

Initially you will probably be treated with suspicion and nobody will think of speaking to the intruder.

Then, one evening, you are likely to overhear a conversation like the one in the P. G. Wodehouse story mentioned here: one beer drinker claiming to remember when the girls were all six feet and two inches tall and boasted more curves than a coastal railway, and that they were now no more than five feet tall and disappeared when seen side on.

A phenomenon he felt to be very strange.

A drinking companion agreed and added that the same thing happens with dogs. One minute the world being full of pugs whilst the next

126-127 At one time women were banned from pubs. Today this rule has been abolished but there are still rigid opening hours: from eleven in the morning to eleven at night on weekdays and from twelve to three and from seven to half past ten on Sundays. There are also strict laws regarding the age of drinkers and even those who merely want to enter and buy a sandwich. You cannot enter a pub and order "a beer" and it is not simply a question of brands. Light ale has little in common with barley wine, pale is not the same as brown ale. And while some may like the sweet flavour of shandy — a blend of lemonade and beer — others may prefer the sharper taste of a pint of old.

there are only pekes and alsatians to be seen. A third drinker added that the matter is all very strange and that we are probably destined never to know the cause.

If at this point you manage to avoid thinking that the spirit of London really is an unfathomable mystery and also manage to avoid the error of interrupting, then perhaps something of this city has already found room in your heart.

128-129 Parliament Street retains its solemn air in the evening. Political power has been at home in this area of London for at least ten centuries, and while the statesmen may come and go and laws and governments may change, Westminster remains the same.

130-131 The London Bridge we see today was built in 1971: this was, however, the site of the city's first bridge built by the Romans in the first century AD when they created their city and port here. Twenty centuries later that small village has expanded into an immense city in which people of all races live together.

136 The royal coat of arms, seen here on the main gate of Buckingham Palace is the symbol of an ancient monarchy. As King Farouk of Egypt said, in the future there will remain but five kings, those in the pack of cards and the King of England.

INDEX